Umbrian Twilight

Tra il Lusco e il Brusco

G I O V A N N A   P I C C O Z Z I

authorHOUSE®

AuthorHouse™
1663 Liberty Drive
Bloomington, IN 47403
www.authorhouse.com
Phone: 1-800-839-8640

Published by AuthorHouse 4/2/2013

ISBN: 978-1-4817-2672-6 (sc)
ISBN: 978-1-4817-2671-9 (hc)
ISBN: 978-1-4817-2673-3 (e)

Library of Congress Control Number: 2013904360

Cover photography by Giovanna Piccozzi, World War I, Memorial, Cortona, Italy.

This book is printed on acid-free paper.

Dedicated to Rinny.

Chapter 1
Awakening

There is that moment when we enter into the twilight of the night, the sun patiently awaiting her glory while the moon gently surrenders its luminosity of the night to the pending day. Time is now a convenience inflicted on humanity. We have it, find it, lose it, and want it. We never really have it. It is merely a man-made perception of reality. This reality truly is a devil's game, a total delight to what we call our dark side. I patiently wait. A thought momentarily appears within the sleepy caverns of my mind. Maybe it is a bridge between the worlds of my soul, the night, and my dream. Perhaps the thought was a dream or a moment of my awakening to reality of the day. It is the moment prior to the mind's taking control, much like the early morning fog in the harbor—a sense of what is there not yet defined within mind or sight. The day has begun.

It's time to go. I must gather my belongings and close the door behind me. Freshness fills the early April morning. The sky appears brilliant blue after the months of winter's monochromatic gray. The walk to the ferry is short and gratefully downhill, the pathway merely a remnant of the stately old Prospect Hotel, which burned down for the second and last time in 1941. It also is a statement of this small, sheltered island. It is a summer haven for cosmopolitans. This broken path now guides the traveler down to the ferry terminal. The terminal once had a magical feeling to it, a strange-shaped shingled building with a simple turnstile. The sound of the approaching ferry echoes up the hill to the crest of this once majestic park. The current ferry terminal is hardly a historic building, the original razed and replaced by cinder block, which someone mistakenly painted violet. The spring air mixes with the salt scent of the harbor, and I think back to my youth. Then a moment of anxiety overtakes me. Did I shut off the electric? Did I lock the door? I'm resolved; it doesn't really matter. I'll call someone later to check. I smile and remember I closed the door behind me.

I board through the turnstile and embark on the *Prospect*, the ferry named after the famous hotel. The old-timers who lived during its heyday are gradually dying off, leaving only faded black-and-white photographs and written history to attest to the *Prospect*'s stateliness. For me, the stories are firsthand from my mother, father, grandmother, and grandfather. They, too, are becoming merely faded memories of a time gone by.

The harbor is still and vacant. The water reflects the blue sky. The ferry ride takes just seven minutes. As the ferry approaches the pier I see two fishing boats are tied at the mainland pier. A flock of seagulls hovers over their sterns—a sign of the fishing vessels' recent return to port. As the ferry approaches, the smell of the fish-hold wafts through the air. The calming seashore smells soon are replaced with the diesel exhaust of the commuter bus parked near the ferry terminal. The awaiting bus will be the second leg of my journey. I disembark and walk over. I hand my bag to the attendant, board, and take my seat. I look around, noticing there are only three other travelers on board. The bus departs, and I drift into sleep.

I awake to hear the attendant announce "airport connection" and realize I have slept the entire ride. I gather my few belongings, still half-asleep, and walk off the bus to the waiting taxi. There are four words to get me home: "JFK Delta terminal two." The taxi driver's name is Max, and he makes small talk as we speed through the traffic. He tells his taxi tales of the day and the adventures of his earlier passengers. I wonder if I will be the topic for his next fare. We pull up to the terminal; I open the door and thank Max for the express ride, stories, and most important, for getting me to the airport on time. I reach the terminal, entering the automatic sliding doors open, and I realize this is my portal home. My foot steps on the white, cool, tiled floor, and I breathe in the familiar smell—jet fuel from yesterday and today, daily planes departing and arriving. I hear the loudspeaker addressing flight departures and arrivals, but I can do this portion of the journey blindfolded. I now have a Cheshire cat smile on my face. I've crossed through St. Peter's gate, and I'm on my way. The ticket counter is vacant of travelers, while three agents stand ready to facilitate check-in. Within a few minutes, I have my boarding pass and head for security. I travel light and simple. Security is less of a hassle, as I travel often and have access to the express medallion line. For me, however, there is always that moment when the security agent looks at my passport, then at me, and then at my passport again. Those detective eyes make me feel as if every sin I have ever committed has somehow been transmitted to him telepathically. I still feel fear racing within me. Only when I get the final nod am I able to release my breath. I admit I don't mind the luggage scan or the walk-through metal detector. That part's easy, except of course for a few Americans who travel with their entire wardrobe and bathroom. I scold myself that it is not for me to judge. I'm now cleared and good to go. Slipping my shoes back on, I grab my bag—one step closer to heaven. I head down to the Travelex booth to change the American greenbacks for some beautiful euros. Today, the airport seems empty. Where is everyone?

I hear my name called over the loud speaker and I am advised to go directly to my gate. The agent greets me and says with a big smile, "This seat will be more comfortable for you, and you may board the aircraft at this time." I look down at the ticket—3A. I've been upgraded. I love Delta. Loyalty has its rewards. I gladly pass my new ticket to the agent at the Jetway and walk down the corridor. The Jetway is lined with duty-free liquor bottles, perfumes, and whatever else Americans just can't live without, each bag tagged with names and flight numbers stapled to the outside.

I am comfortable traveling alone. If anything reinforces my independence, it's being a single mother of five. As I cross through the threshold of the cabin, the flight attendant glances at my ticket and directs me to my seat. I stow my small carry-on overhead and nestle into my deluxe business-class seat.

The flight attendant offers a choice of champagne or juice. The choice is simple for me—champagne. The young man sitting next to me smiles and asks for juice.

I'm now sitting in the airplane on the tarmac of New York's JFK Airport, waiting to go home. Home is a long and twisted path for me. Home is a farmhouse in Umbria, Italy. Home is my solitude and my haven. How is it that I am brought to this moment? How is it that it takes approximately five thousand miles to bring me home? Before I am allowed to answer this question for myself, a voice comes over the loudspeaker.

"Passengers, my name is Captain Atwood."

It doesn't really matter what his name is. To me, it is a mere formality and a voice of assurance to the novice traveler. I don't pay any attention. Time seems to be altered, and I realize my Delta Airline flight has been sitting on the tarmac longer than usual; my flight has been delayed. I wonder what this delay means. Poor weather conditions in Roma or heavy air traffic? I am going home, and that is all that matters. The young man sitting next to me appears to be a veteran traveler as well, and we smile and continue minding our own business.

If your flight is going to be delayed, the only place to be is in business class. I appreciate this privilege. I am well aware of what it is like to be incarcerated in the steerage area of a plane, with or without a delay. International flights are either overbooked or barren, and there is no apparent reason for the pattern. I've seen planes full during holidays as well as completely empty. I can only surmise that it is all in the order of the universe. I will tell you up front that I believe in the power of the universe, probably more than most. Somewhere along my life's journey, our church's priest, Father Peter, said, "God's here to help with the big problems, so don't worry about them."

So the universe or God is in charge, now and always. Even Einstein stated he wanted to know how God made this universe. Captain Atwood's voice again comes over the PA system. He assures us we will depart shortly. I don't have a connecting flight, so the delay is a mere inconvenience. I'll have another glass of champagne to celebrate my journey.

Somewhere in the caverns of my mind, I hear, "We will be refueling."

Refueling? What does this mean? Not life-threatening; the problem is simple. The plane has exhausted its fuel reserve for the journey across the Atlantic. The plane must now return to a designated refueling area. Bravo to the astute flight engineer. We won't run out of fuel over France. I glance over at my new traveling companion and smile. The plane's taxi is a confused series of turns. Looking out the window, I am not sure if my eyes are telling me the truth as to where the plane is headed or if we are under some crazy government surveillance.

I look at the young man sitting next to me and say, "I think they are taking us to a security check area rather than a refueling location."

He looks at me with a strange smile and nods his head. I am transformed, back to seventeen years of age, wide-eyed. The world was not Twain's *Innocents Abroad*, nor Aristophanes' *Clouds* or Plato's *Republic*. It had now become my Peloponnesian War.

I'm sitting next to this young man, so why are the scholars I sought in the past now beckoning me? This flight has become a revisit to a classic *Twilight Zone* episode. My mind now has the best of me. I am grateful there still exists a mind to haunt me.

I long to remember my favorite verse from *Clouds*. It will come to me. I think of the universe, and I am lost in thought.

The plane's video system is still inactive, and we have yet to view the safety video. Apparently, the system needs to be rebooted, so we sit. Reading just doesn't seem to fit my mood or mind-set at this moment. The smell of jet fuel is intoxicating, much like a birthday cake in the oven or a roasting Thanksgiving turkey—events where the anticipation is more stimulating than the actual celebration. I realize this journey will take longer than anticipated, but the plane is full of wine and food, and the night is still young. Normally, if you sit in business class, people want to know "nothing about nothing"; not who you are, not where you're from—absolutely nothing. Basically, the only questions or answers you will hear are, "What wine and what entree have you decided for today?" I decide to break the silence and the unspoken business-class rule.

"Where are you going?" I ask.

"To Roma" was his short reply, with no follow-up.

"Are you going for business or pleasure?"—my second feeble attempt to start a conversation.

He produced a short sigh with what appeared to be a second sigh of resignation on his part. "I'm actually working now," he said.

My immediate thought was, *He works for Delta and is on his way back to Roma, either to work at the Fuminciano Airport or travel on another flight to a distant location.* "What do you do for Delta?" I ask.

He replies, "I don't work for Delta. I'm a US marshal. I'm here to protect the plane in the event of any incident."

This was not the comforting response I was hoping to hear. What did he mean by "an incident"? Yet with that said, I realize the flight and I are in secure hands. I ask myself why a simple flight home requires a marshal. Have we, as a planet, all gone mad? Is this the *Twilight Zone* episode where a passenger keeps seeing a creature on the wing of the plane, and everyone on board thinks he's crazy, but when the plane lands, there is an enormous gash ripped from the skin of the wing? Then the realization of September 11 floods my mind. I'm sitting with a man who defends national and international security, and my feeling of comfort wanes. I decide to restore our brief conversation to take my mind off any pending anxiety.

"How long will you stay in Roma?" I ask.

"Just two days, and then I head back to the US."

"Do you ever have the opportunity to stay longer and travel into the country or visit other cities?"

"Not often. The job is more or less back-and-forth. Sometimes, if I know the flight crew, I will spend time with them in Roma. But most of the time I just stay at the airport hotel to catch up on some lost sleep and relax."

At this point I thought we should introduce ourselves. I asked, "So what's your name, and where are you from?"

"The name is Mike, and I'm from Pennsylvania. I prefer working out of New York. It's actually easier for me to get in and out of New York than it is to deal with getting in and out of Washington, DC, and there are more flights to choose from. I prefer the nonstop flights, making New York the best choice. I like the flight to Roma; it's not too long, and I can easily go into the city if I want to have fun. The hotel shuttle is free, runs often, and stops right at Victor Emanuel. What's your name, and where do you live? What are you doing on this flight, and where are you going?"

He had asked all the basic questions in one quick sentence. I could hear that Pennsylvania accent, and I could certainly see he knew how to line up the questions in one simple breath.

Over the PA system the captain announces, "We will be departing shortly."

Mike and I look at each other with a nod and a roll of the eyes. We've heard that before. "Shortly," in aviation terms, means anything under an hour.

"My name is Giovanna. In America, the name is Joann.

7

Italians don't have a J in their alphabet. When I first arrived in Italy seven years ago, I told everyone, 'My name is Joann,' and they immediately responded, 'Giovanna.' So when in Italy, I am Giovanna, and in the United States, Joann. I live on eastern Long Island, on a small island between the two forks, as the locals fondly call them. You have to take a ferry to get there. It's quiet in the winter, and it's a resort madhouse in the summer. When the first cool winds blow, I try to make my escape. I always say I'm going home. I think of Italy as my home and the States as a place to visit. But someday, Italy will be my home; it already has my soul. Right now, the reason is mere economics and reality."

"So why do you fly to Roma?" he asks, looking at me inquisitively.

"I own a farm in the countryside between Florence and Roma on the Tuscan/Umbria border. The farm has ten hectares of land, and a local farmer farms the larger fields, and I work with my neighbors to harvest the olives for olive oil. The town is extremely small; I believe the last census count was 304 people. This is an inflated census, as I have heard of only one birth but know of three deaths. Italy is one of the few countries in the world with a zero or negative population growth."

Mike looked at me with confusion. "How did you get to buy a farm in Italy—or more important, why did you make that decision?"

I thought I could start with the abridged version, which is fairly generic in nature, but Captain Atwood came over the PA system. "We are now ready for takeoff, and the flight crew should prepare the cabin."

Taking off and landing are my favorite parts of this segment of my journey. The views are so astounding. I look over at Mike. He does look like the stereotypical marshal—late twenties, crew cut, and the body of an athlete. His attire affords him the liberty to blend into any situation. I think, *does he have a gun under that jacket?*

Captain Atwood again makes an announcement. This time

his voice is agitated. "This plane will not take off until the passenger using his cell phone shuts it off!"

Now, if ever I thought there might be a riot on a plane, it was now. Whoever was using a cell phone certainly could lose his or her life—the arrogant passenger who believes he or she need not heed the request to shut off the phone. *What could possibly be so important?* I think. *Can this individual believe he will save a life or the world if he stays on the phone for one more minute?* I look at Mike and say, "Your services might be needed in a moment."

His face lightens up and an enormous smile appears. "That's what I'm here for."

The flight attendant comes over to take our dinner and drink order. We have had the liberty of drinks and snacks while sitting for hours on the tarmac. We place our dinner request. The flight attendant informs us that she will return shortly, before departure, to pick up our glasses.

I look at Mike and say, "I guess you can't have a glass of wine while on duty, can you?"

"No, it's fine. I save that for the evening, when I can relax and enjoy Italy, knowing everyone has arrived safely."

We are comfortable, but the agony of the economy class passengers starts to creep into my mind. "Don't you just think they could serve something to the passengers in the back of the plane? I travel often and often in the back of the plane. Why do we get drinks and get pampered, while three-quarters of the plane sits parched?"

Mike looks at me. "I think you travel this airline as much as I and probably more than most people on the plane. We often are sitting back there, so I know what you mean. It's disheartening; there should be an in-between class—lower business, upper economy. But when we get the upgrade, we feel guilty in some way. We feel guilty because we feel compassion for our fellow passengers incarcerated in steerage. I know I am always grateful when they overbook a flight, simply because I know an upgrade

9

is pending. I wait for that moment just before boarding the plane, and I hope to hear my name called out over the PA system."

I respond quickly, "That doesn't mean there shouldn't be something between whitewashing a fence and painting the Annunciation."

Mike bursts out laughing and quickly, the woman in front of us turns around with a look of contempt. "Now tell me your story," he says. "We have a long flight ahead of us."

"It's a long story. You might get bored," I say.

"Most stories are long and usually, the longer the better. We have seven hours."

"I'll tell you my story. You tell me yours." I am not sure if I am lightheaded from the champagne; the moment is ours. I look at Mike and say, "Are you sure you are ready for my tale?"

Again, his face lights up with a smile and with a laugh. "I've checked the movies that are available, and I've seen them all, so your story will do just fine and I'm sure it will be more interesting than most of the B-rated movies the flight has to offer."

Well, here we go. ...

"In 1974 I spent the summer in Italy and Greece."

Mike breaks in. "Did you fall in love?"

I smile. "I was seventeen. Yes, I fell in love but, strangely, with a Greek. He was a young man who worked at the hotel where we stayed while studying ancient art and literature. He was a hoot, if you know what I mean. But I stray from my Italian journey. Let me get back on track to my sojourn in Italy, approximately ten or so years ago, Oh, wait a minute—I do remember the year. George H. Bush was elected president!" I burst out laughing, adding, "I hope you're not a Republican. I decided it was time to return to Italy. There is nothing unusual about this. Every young woman who travels to Italy falls in love, either with an Italian man or the country itself. Somehow, I guess I never really lost that love for Italy and her people. One of my missions in Italy was to locate my father's family. They came from a small town near the Adriatic called Popoli. I wanted to see if Italy really was in my heart and soul and if I could fall back in love as I had thirty years ago, when I first went there and found peace. Remember, I was a seventeen-year-old girl back then. The basic goal of the second trip was to fly into Nice, France, and drive south along the Mediterranean and down the Italian coast. I would make my journey across the country to Popoli. I made no reservations; I had simply rented a car and brought a map. The only specific destination was Popoli."

"Mike, have you traveled through Italy?"

"I have been up to Florence and Venice. Florence is beautiful and a great city. Venice is different. I'm not sure I can say I was taken by her charm. I would say it was her uniqueness that intrigued me the most. I'm sorry to say it was more like visiting Disney—everyone there seemed to be a tourist and it lost its charm for me."

The plane finally has reached its cruising altitude. The seat belt sign is now turned off. The captain makes an announcement, telling us that we are free to move about the cabin, but we are not free to loiter or gather in the aisles, "Federal aviation rules."

I look over at Mike and say, "This is your job, preventing passengers from loitering or gathering in the aisles?"

We both laugh. Mike says, "You'd be amazed how many people actually try to smoke in the bathrooms. They are easy to identify. It is normally during the 'sleepy time' of the flight, when even the attendants are catching some rest. A rogue passenger will slip into the restroom and have a smoke. I admit they are pretty clever at covering the smoke detectors, but they stink like smoke when they come out."

Mike begins to tell me a little bit more about his life. When he'd finished college, job prospects were slim. He thought of joining the armed forces but had second thoughts. Then someone mentioned that Mike could qualify for a federal job— the government was hiring, and a federal job would assure him an income and benefits, and he could travel. He enjoyed living in rural Pennsylvania, where there was a certain peace to the countryside and not the frenzied lifestyle of a city. He claimed to be a good old country boy with a college education and a love for travel. I thought the "good old country boy" part just didn't fit. He was well educated with some upper-class finishing touches. I imagined he was the heartthrob of every girl in his small, rural Pennsylvania town.

The flight attendant walks down the aisle and hands each of us a warm towel to clean our hands, the official signal that drink and dining is about to begin. We clean ourselves up and on cue; the next steward comes by to collect our soiled towels.

"So tell me more about your Italian journey," Mike says.

I realize I really like this young man; he is genuine and probably lonely. "Okay, if you want, I will humor you but you must promise you will tell me to stop when you're bored or you could just pretend to fall asleep."

He nods his affirmation.

"Well, it was the best journey. In fact, it taught me what I had learned and what I had forgot. Does that make sense to you?"

"It actually does. Well put."

"I would travel during the morning and find a small town to stay in. Afternoons in Italy are my favorites. The towns are quiet, everyone is home having lunch, and there is a tranquility one can sense in the sunlight and the buildings. I always managed to find one small café open that would serve wine and a panini. I had nothing more to want. The piazzas were filled with life, even though they were emptied for siesta. Voices seemed to come from behind the shuttered windows; smells of lunch cooking filled the air. I had a sense of being fulfilled and satisfied. I love the Italian countryside. To me, it doesn't matter if you are sitting alone in a piazza or walking down a street alone; in Italy, you are never alone. It's like the souls of everyone walk with you. You know what it's really like? It's that feeling you get when you think of your grandmother—something gentle and kind with a certain scent and a certain light." I look over to see if he is awake.

Much to my surprise, he is awake and smiling. "It's funny that you say that," he says, "that feeling of not being alone in Italy. I have that feeling of thinking of someone who throughout my life may have comforted me but isn't here today ... yet still is." Now his smile is full of grace and fulfillment, a smile that is from his heart and soul. After a moment he asks, "Did you ever find Popoli?"

"Yes, I found Popoli. I found my heart and soul as well."

Mike's smile broadens. "This sounds like a romance is about to happen."

I laugh. "No romance, actually, just peace. I have five children, and having a romance is not what I was looking for, at least not at that moment of my life. I've been a single mom for more than twenty years. Romance for me is being with my friends, and having a great dinner, and laughing the night away. Finding a sense of home and serenity was my quest. My children thought I was completely crazy when I returned home and said I was buying a house in Italy. I believe it was Corinne, my third child, who just cracked up laughing. Actually, I thought she would wet her pants because she could not contain herself, but she somehow managed to say, 'Mom, you don't even speak Italian. What are you going to do in Italy?'" I laughed along with her as I remembered that obvious hurdle I had overlooked. My only response to her, as we both were bent over in laughter, was, 'I learned to speak French; I can learn to speak Italian.' Then my son said, 'What are you going to do in Italy? You can't work there. You can't stay there for more than three months. Are you also planning on becoming an Italian citizen?' The one and only son is the old sage of the family. I thought about that question for a split second and then told him, 'I'll figure that out when it's time, and besides, I believe in Zen.'"

"Sounds like your kids were the protective parent, and

you were the teenager," Mike says, laughing. "By the way, did Corinne wet her pants?"

"No, but from that day on, my dear sweet children came up with their term of endearment for me: 'Crazy Lady.' The name still sticks to this day. When they think I've temporarily lost my mind—which, by the way, is often—my daughter Zoe will say 'Hey, Crazy Lady, did you really just do that?' We have a great relationship. I think the single-parenting thing worked for all of us. They didn't have the opportunity to pit one parent against the other. However, they developed some keen techniques for getting their way at times. Here is one of my favorites: Corinne—I nicknamed her Rin or Rinny—wanted to go with a friend after school. During my waking hours, I said no. Well, they all knew when I was asleep, I was sound asleep, but I could be woken to a faint sense of consciousness. So Rin had put a note together that basically gave my permission for her to go to a friend's house after school. Then she asked me to sign it—I was sleeping, remember, but I signed it. The next day, I came home from work, looked around, and asked, 'Where's Rin?' Everyone started laughing. Finally, Zoe said, 'You signed the note.' I didn't know what she was talking about. 'What note?' I asked. And Zoe responded, 'The note that said Rin could go to her friend's house. You signed it this morning … while you were still sleeping.'"

Mike looks amazed. "Did you get mad?"

"Nope. I have this strong belief that if you are faced with an obstacle and you can figure it out, bravo for you. The other golden rule is the no-yelling rule. Parents are always yelling at their children and children yell at their parents. Everyone yells and no one listens—that's the standard. When I do get mad, I just give my evil-eye look and walk away. Being silent is much more successful than the verbal thrashing. But the best part is, it really works."

"So you give the evil eye and walk away? Can you really do that?"

I start to laugh and say, "How do you think I raised five children as a single mom? When I was mad, they knew it. I would not utter a sound to the offending individual. After about two hours, he or she was sorry, made things right, and then we could move on. It didn't work every time, but I would say 90 percent of the time. So that was the response of my children to my purchasing a house and moving to Italy. I guess I really hadn't thought through the logistics of my Italian adventure. I had a quest, and I would achieve my goal of buying a farm in Italy."

Our appetizers arrive, and we eat in silence for a while. Then I ask Mike if he has any children or a wife. He laughs so hard I think he is going to choke on a piece of food.

"Children and a wife are not in my current lifestyle. I travel too much and don't feel that it would be a great foundation for any relationship. It is similar to what you said when I asked if you went to Italy looking for romance, and you said that was not your quest. I do have a dog. Does that count for something?"

Looking him straight in the face, I say, "I hope it's not a little one that you dress up in clothing with a name something along the lines of Cupcake."

"No, his name is Jack, and he's an elkhound, okay? Is that manly enough for you?"

We both laugh hysterically. We are getting a little too loud. We were just having a little fun, but the flight attendant comes down the aisle and asks if we could please talk quietly so as not to disturb the other travelers.

I look at Mike and say, "You are going to be the first marshal to get kicked off of a plane."

Chapter 2
Getting There

Mike dozes off. I pick up the *Financial Times* and look at the date—April 22. Now over the Atlantic, it is April 23. I am brought back to April 23, 1982. ...

It was a record cold day, and the snow outside our home on the island was piling up, blanketing the early spring flowers. I was in labor with my third child. My husband made the call to my sister, asking if she could watch the children. She said she would be right over. Shortly, she arrives and my husband and I began our drive, the roads were slippery, and the ferry seemed to take forever to start up. This being my third child, I knew labor would be fast. My husband sped to the hospital and within half an hour of arriving, Rinny, our third child, was born. She was perfect in every way. Corinne Lenora was named both for Aunt Lena (one of my dad's older sisters) and for my husband's love of the name. My parents were away in Europe, visiting with my oldest sister's in-laws. Eventually, we were able to make contact, and the news of their new grandchild was carried across the Atlantic.

My father said, "Another girl?"

I said, "Yes, and don't forget I did give you the first grandson."

He laughed.

Rinny grew into a miniature Aunt Lena. Rin could cook before she could read. She loved to garden and to be outside. Animals were another of her loves. Horses would soon learn her talent as a rider and gentle trainer. The yearning for a horse in her life was impossibly strong. She worked at barns—giving pony rides, mucking stables, anything to be near horses—and she would trade her labor for riding lessons. When she wasn't at the barn, she would read profusely—anything and everything connected to horses. Her birthday and Christmas wish lists were always the same: a horse.

I struggle hard to remember all of the events in her life—learning to drive, learning to ride a horse, learning to swim. It was all coming back to me. Rin and her brother Tyrus were inseparable. They slept in the same room well into their early teens, always sure an alien spaceship was outside their window—at least that was the story confirmed by both as a reason to share the same bedroom and be together. I think the real reason was that they both were untidy children. Each bed was piled so high with random items; I'm not sure how they climbed in at night.

My flashback moves forward. Dark clouds cover the stars; the day switches to July 17, 1999. ...

The day was hot muggy and the night as calm and eerie as in a Fellini movie. We had just moved back to the island from New Hampshire. The day was spent getting organized, as many of the last few weeks had been. It was time for bed. I had fallen asleep on the sofa. Everyone was playing and singing. There was a kiss and a soft-spoken voice that said, "I love you. It's time to go to bed." It was Rinny. I woke, realizing that I had fallen asleep on the sofa.

Nodding my head in agreement, I returned the kiss and moved to the bedroom upstairs. "I love you too."

Rinny smiled.

I was exhausted from relocating to the island and starting a new job. This was not a small challenge, but everyone pitched in and made the best of it. Morning came; the sun was shining. I was slow to leave the haven of bed and slumber, even as the day called. I looked out over the fields next to the house. My car was down the driveway, and Rinny was on the passenger side. I thought, *she's late for work. What is she doing? What did she forget?*

It took me one more moment ... and then my life turned upside down. I went to call her name from the open window, but lightning ran through my body. Something was not right. The car was pinned against the tree, and Rinny was not moving. I felt paralyzed, fear-filled with pain, yet I had to move. I had to run down those stairs and out across the lawn. Maybe I was wrong, I called her name, but there was only the silence of the morning. I called 911.

The women on the other end of the phone talked and talked. "Stay on the line; stay on the line. I wanted to throw the phone down on the kitchen counter; I wanted to be with her. The woman's voice calmly said. "Help is on its way."

I didn't know. I couldn't answer. I needed help, and I needed to be with my daughter. I heard the sirens coming from far away, and as they approached, the sound was deafening, and then the flashing red lights pulled into the driveway. Rinny would no longer be here. I had to reach the other children. They were asleep in the house. How could I keep them from waking to the horrible sirens and flashing lights? There is no logic or sense at times such as these. My universe—the one that takes care—was now not quite big enough to help. Somehow, I had to wake them and say what was impossible to say or believe: "Your sister Rinny is dead."

Suddenly, I am back on the plane, cabin lights dim, and the roar of the engines seems overwhelming. I pull myself back from this nightmare, hating to be in that thought. I look long and hard to find all the joyous moments we had together. I think Aunt Lena and Rinny are in a kitchen somewhere, cooking and laughing. I also think of a paddock full of horses, with Rinny riding majestically. I assure myself she is still here in my heart and in the hearts of many. The last tear rolls down my face, and the smile of the last good-night kiss comforts me. I look now at the journey, thinking of the peace of Italy. But that moment of waking my children to face what I could not face will never pass. There cannot be a moment in one's life when you wake your children to tell them their sister is gone. I need to think of something that will remove this sadness from my mind. I smile and think of my first trip to my farm to pick olives in early November. ...

I'd taken a direct Swiss Air flight to Zurich from JFK Airport. The adventure started with my taking the train from Zurich down to Florence. I would then drive down to my farm, Olivetta. The journey seemed more in keeping with my perception of a traditional Italian lifestyle. Why fly directly from New York to Roma when I could take the night train to Florence? This certainly was a romantic notion on my part, but all romantic notions do have twists and turns. Mine was starting at the Zurich train station. The layover between plane arrival and train departure was ten hours. I decided to check my bag and explore Zurich. I handed my bag over to the baggage-check gentleman; he smiled and handed me my receipt. Off I went. I wandered along the canal, walked through the crowded flea market, and decided it was time to find a local bar. As fate would have it, as if on cue, the local establishment of my dreams appeared—dark and filled with Swiss; not a tourist in sight. This was my first time in Zurich. I asked in my broken French for a glass of red wine. The bartender smiled and then took a glass and a bottle of wine from the shelf. He poured the wine, level with a small etched line on the side of the glass, just about an inch from the bottom. I thought he must want me to try the wine to see if I liked it. I was wrong. That was, in fact, all the wine that would be forthcoming in this glass. I imaged that this etched line had to do with the Swiss being so precise—there would be no over-pour.

I smiled, paid him, and took a sip. Soon, I was befriended by the three young gentlemen who were sitting to my left. We exchanged tales in English, and the afternoon slipped away. It was time for dinner, and my three new friends assured me that our dinner would be at a wonderful local restaurant, a five-minute trolley ride away. I expected to purchase a ticket once we were on the trolley, but I soon discovered that only tourists do that. The locals merely jump on the back of the slow-moving trolley until they arrive at the desired destination, and then they jump off.

The restaurant was small and full of voices and music. The menu was fondue—just fondue—along with more wine and more laughter. I have never seen so much fondue at one table in my entire life. And yet we managed to consume it all.

Time soon reared its ugly head. I would miss my train if we did not leave immediately. We settled the bill and ran to fetch the trolley. We all jumped back on the trolley and went to the train station and then to the baggage pickup area.

Well, the baggage area had closed thirty minutes prior to our arrival, but I could not miss my train. I had to be down at the farm for the olive harvest. I had absolutely nothing with me but my wallet and passport. Everything else was secured in the baggage area. I needed to make a decision. In total trust, I decided I would give my three new friends the baggage claim ticket and money to cover the cost of the baggage claim. They would return to the station two weeks from now at 8 a.m. to meet me and produce my travel bag. With kisses and laughter, we bid our good-byes. I boarded the night train and walked into my sleeper. The darkness of the Swiss sky was unearthly—I felt as if I was in outer space, looking at stars light-years away. Content, I dozed off.

I arrived in Florence early the next morning. I collected myself, as I had no belongings, and left to find the car rental agency. Having worn the same clothing for over twenty-four hours, I was sure the car rental agent must think I was a vagabond. I made my way through the usual pile of documents and stamps, and the car keys finally were handed over. I merely had to locate the car in a huge parking lot, with no exact designation for an aisle or a parking slot. Using the unlock button was the only way I ever found the car. Now I was ready to head off to Olivetta and harvest my olives.

The Autostrada, the name for Italy's superhighway, is more like an advanced video racecar game than a highway, but there are rules, and they are always followed. One never drives in the left lane with the exception of passing. The left blinker must remain on until you return to the right lane—this allows other drivers to understand you are still continuing at unreasonably high speeds in order to pass, and you have no intention of slowing down quite yet. The headlights must always be on, and the minimum speed is 140 km/h (kilometers per hour). This is understood instinctively, though the correct speed is 130 km/h. Speed is monitored by an electronic velocity—*il limite di velocita*—camera. The amusement is that drivers are notified well in advance that such a device is ahead, and only unsuspecting tourists are caught in the electronic speed trap.

A stop at the Autogrill was mandatory. I silently reminded myself that I was traveling at excessive speeds and needed to have my wits about me. It took one cappuccino to refresh me. No one seems to be able to pass up a stop at an Autogrill while traversing the Autostrada. The drive south was beautiful. Small hilltop towns dotted the horizon, the occasional Eurostar—fast-train—flashed by. Its speed was amazing. I was driving at 130 km/h, and the Eurostar passed me as if I were standing still.

Large tractor-trailer trucks moved in a deliberate single file. The caravan of trucks looked more like a caterpillar than a single line of independent trucks. Their maximum and minimum speed limits were posted on the back of each truck. Speed limits for trucks are strictly enforced, the maximum/minimum based on whether they are carrying a load or traveling empty.

A black BMW or Mercedes passed me at the speed of light. I

always had to remember that while driving in Italy, I must look in the rearview mirror as frequently as I looked through the front windshield, as cars seemed to appear out of nowhere. Very few Autostrada exits in Italy were numbered. An exit consisted of a town's name, along with another fifty other small town possible options. The Chiusi exit—my exit—appeared. The exit served approximately thirty small towns, and if I missed the exit, I might well find myself at the end of Italy's boot while still looking for my exit. I took the exit ramp and pulled up to the tollbooth. On my right were two *Carabinieri* (federal officers), one with a machine gun and the other with a small white stick with a red circle on the end. As I pulled away from the tollbooth, the Carabinieri raised the small stick. I knew that when the tiny stick was raised, it was time to pull over and await one's fate. He approached the car and began speaking in very fast Italian. I immediately informed him in my basic Italian that I spoke little Italian … and then there was a silence. After a moment, he informed me in broken English that I must use my headlights while on the Autostrada. I knew this; how could I have forgotten to turn the headlights on while driving? Then with a stern yet gentle smile, he waved me on.

The Carabinieri are more like federal agents than police officers. One very important fact to know is that you must never touch the Carabinieri, not even a tap on the shoulder.

I remembered my friend Robert telling me his story. "I was in the Termini train station," he'd said, "attempting to find my way to the platform from which I was to depart. I looked at the departure board but didn't see my train or the word *Chiusi*. The station was ten times crazier than Grand Central Station in New York City. I looked around, but no one from Tranitalia was anywhere to be found. The only agent I found did not speak English. My mom and dad always said that if I ever needed help, I should ask a police officer. I thought the Carabinieri were police officers."

I'd asked him, "Robert, don't you know who the Italian

Carabinieri are? They are as close to an FBI agent as anyone could imagine. Please don't tell me you actually touched him."

"How was I to know they were an Italian version of a federal agent?" he'd responded. "A group of Carabinieri was talking, and they were ignoring me and my attempt to ask for directions. I thought I could just tap one on the shoulder, and he would turn and help me. What he did was look at me with distain and turn his back to me. There was absolutely no possible way I was going to receive any assistance from them."

I laughed to myself, remembering my own Carabinieri story. I was at a flea market in Arezzo with my friends Pietro and Sarah. We were looking for furniture for Olivetta, my farmhouse. At one point, two Carabinieri approached Pietro and begin speaking Italian. Next to them was a film crew. They spoke to Pietro for what seemed an eternity, as Sarah and I looked on. The only time I'd heard a Carabinieri speak was at the tollbooth at the Chiusi exit. Why was a film crew traveling with them, and why had they stopped us? After much (or as the Italians say, *man mano*) conversation, Pietro explained that the Carabinieri wanted to improve their image and wanted to make a video of two people asking for assistance.

I looked at Pietro and Sarah, completely confused. "They want to make a public relations film with us?"

Pietro and Sarah laughed. Their joint reply was *si*. Knowing what I knew about the Carabinieri, I was more than confused. Pietro looked at me and said we would do it together. "You are an English-speaking woman. I am an Italian, trying to understand you. They will provide the solution to the problem."

His only communication to me in English was, "Giovanna, just remember to smile." Sarah, on the other hand, tried not to bust a gut with laughter. The result: Pietro and I and two Carabinieri had a conversation in English and Italian—and eventually we were seen somewhere on public television in Italy.

One major Italian rule—never touch a Carabinieri. If you try to catch the Carabinieri's attention and they ignore you, it is best to just move on. If you try to get their attention with a tap on the shoulder, they will ignore you and continue their conversation among themselves.

The drive to Villastrada from Chiusi was picture book perfect.

Chiusi itself is one of the twelve major Etruscan centers in Italy. This old city sits perched on a hill. Its ancient wall protects the city today, as it has for thousands of years. Etruscan caves are dotted along the hills and buried beneath the city's shops.

I continued along the winding, hilly road. The olive groves were full of people. Ladders were nestled in the olive trees, and individuals seemed precariously perched on ladder and branches. I passed over the small bridge that divided Tuscany from Umbria.

There are two towers, a statement by each region. The Tuscans built their tower first, saying to the Umbrians, "Take this," to which the Umbrians replied, "Take that." constructing a tower twice as large. To this day, the Umbrians are proud of their impressive tower and their perceived superiority over Tuscans.

As I continued to drive, I saw the rusted and creased blue-and-white lettered sign for Villastrada. I was home. The road curved and rose for another kilometer and then suddenly, the market appeared on the right. I stopped at the stop sign and looked cautiously—the drivers in this small town traveled as if this were an extension of the Autostrada, though the road was barely a car and a half wide. I turned just after the market and just before the post office onto my driveway. The driveway was narrow, nestled between a small house and the back of the *macellerea* (market). I passed by my neighbor Paolo's home. As always, Paolo would be sitting either outside, looking over the fields, or working in his small but extremely productive vegetable garden. On this day he was working in the garden. I stopped and bade him the morning greetings and then continued on my way. It was at this point the driveway's pavement ended, and it turned sharply to the left, winding along the vineyards and olive groves. Straight ahead was Olivetta, my small Italian farmhouse. ...

I'm startled from sleep—dreaming or hallucinating—by the flight attendant, who asks if we would care for dessert and an after-dinner cordial.

I look at Mike and ask, "Was I snoring or talking in my sleep?"

He looks as confused as I. "I don't know. I think I must have been sleeping, because I remember being someplace else." he utters. "I think we both were someplace else," It takes him a minute to actually understand where he is and who the crazy lady is sitting next to him.

"Any good dreams you want to share?" I ask.

"I think I was dreaming about being on your olive farm."

I want to ask him just how old he is. I'm not sure why I'm curious; I certainly was not planning on seducing a marshal on his way to Italy.

"You can come to Olivetta whenever you're in town," I tell him. "It's easy. You take the fast train from Roma and get off at Chiusi. It takes about an hour and a half. If you want, you can come up to the farmhouse with me now, and I can drive you to the station when you have to go back."

I'm doing what I always do and what my children always tell me not to do. I invite people to my home all the time. If people don't have a place to sleep for whatever reason, I invite them to be comfortable. I can hear my children laughing now, "You can't just keep inviting people to stay with us."

Mike looks at me for a moment and says, "Really?"

"Of course, really, I don't say things I don't mean, and I mean what I say. It's another rule. The weather is supposed to be perfect. I'll take you to my favorite secret spots. I travel alone so much that it would be perfect to have someone travel with me. And it will be fun to have a man to travel with, like having a secret-agent man as my buddy. What do you think?"

"Sounds great, but I think I've known you for maybe six hours and three-quarters of a dinner."

"So what is your point? What does that have to do with seeing the Italian countryside?"

The flight attendant brings our dessert and cordial. Mike asks her if a friend of his, who is a flight attendant, is working on our flight. The flight attendant says that his friend was on yesterday's flight and will be in Roma when we arrive. At this point, we all introduce ourselves. The flight attendant's name is Jasmine, and she has been working for eight years with Delta. I ask how long she will be in Roma, and she tells me three days. I look at Mike and then at Jasmine.

"Well, I'm trying to get Mike to come to the country. Maybe I can convince you both to come. April in the country is the perfect time of the year." As I explained to Mike, I tell Jasmine I can show her the secret villages of the Umbrian/Tuscany countryside.

Someone behind us pushes the attendant call button, and Jasmine excuses herself.

I look at Mike and say, "Why not? You're a marshal. Certainly you can protect yourself in the Italian countryside, and besides, there really is no official police force in the county. What I mean is, the Carabinieri are in Chiusi and Cast del Lago, but only when necessity calls do they venture out into the countryside. Anyway, think about it. If not now, maybe you can come some other time."

"I'll think about it." He smiles that smile.

I reflect for a moment, remembering where I left off in my dream, only now it is a reality. I look at Mike and say, "Do you want to hear more about my Italian adventures?"

"That certainly helps this trip pass by a little quicker for me."

"All right … my first olive harvest. I was just thinking about it when you dozed off."

I had forgotten I was arriving to harvest my olives without actual knowledge of the harvesting process—absolutely none. I drove the car up to the farmhouse, looked over to the fields, and realized I was in a business suit. I was going to walk up to my new neighbors, Rose and Stefano, and say, "*Ciao. Come sta?* I'm here to pick olives." This would certainly play poorly. Thoughts ran through my mind. Would they think I was a complete idiot or just *pazzo, pazzo* (crazy)—an American dressed up to pick olives? Well, there was no time better than the present to face my fears. I parked the car next to the house and walked down the steep, narrow path into the olive grove. The path reminded me of an American Indian footpath, the type depicted in old black-and-white films, certainly not something Italian. Down into the olive grove I went. Rose was the first to greet me. She was up on a ladder in an olive tree. She looked down at me and smiled. I immediately told her in my broken Italian, "I have lost my luggage." Everyone burst into laughter. I had passed the first test. Rose came down from the ladder and showed me the most effective olive-harvesting technique.

Now, there is a degree of animosity between northern and southern Italians. For most Italians, Roma is the dividing line between North and South, much like the Mason-Dixon line divides North and South in the United States. As a result, northern Italians still pick their olives by hand, claiming the southern Italians have become lazy by using a *macchina* (a machine) to pull the olives from the tree or by laying their nets under the trees and letting nature take its course. This laying of the nets simply means that as the olives ripen and fall to the ground, they will be caught in the net. I would learn, under the guidance of Rose and Stefano, to be a northern Italian olive harvester. I took my jacket off and placed it on a *cassetti* (a container) and rolled up my sleeves. It was time to learn how to properly harvest olives.

"*Attenzione a testa sua*. (Mind your head), Giovanna," Stefano said, warning me of the impending danger of olives about to fall on my head. Yet much more dangerous were the large branches being sawed from the trees. Stefano cut small-tree-size branches and threw them to the ground. This, to the novice, could be a possibly fatal blow—or at least result in the loss of an eye. Laughter resonated throughout the trees and fields. *Scala alto, scala basso* (up the ladder, down the ladder)—Stefano probably did this a thousand times a day while harvesting. Then Sonya, Rose and Stefano's daughter, and her friend Carlos arrived. They carried with them their ladder, nets, and *cassetti*. They went off to start working on the next tree. I, being the novice, was denied access to the sacred *scala* (ladder) and the stairway to the treasured fruit. I was to remain picking the lower branches and help pull in the nets, careful not to lose one of the green and purple oval treasures. Rose insisted I have lunch with them. I informed her that I did not eat *carne* (meat). She looked at me in disbelief and then called my other neighbor, Victor, over from his olive grove. She asked Victor to make sure she had understood me correctly.

He asked me the question in Italian, and I answered. Then he asked the question in French and then in broken English. Finally, he confirmed with Rose that I did not eat meat.

Rose looked at me and then at Victor, asking him to ask me if I ate chicken.

I looked at her and Victor and said, "*Grazie, no*." Well, no one fell off the ladder or out of the tree, so I figured I was now home free.

Then Rose looked at Stefano and told him to go to the market before it closed. "Giovanna will need mozzarella with her lunch. And pick more tomatoes from the garden."

Off Stefano went, as instructed by Rose. There were no questions asked when Rose was in charge.

The church bells tolled, and we were off to lunch. The church bells were the official timekeepers for this small town. They guided everyone through their daily routines. First, though, we had to collect the nets and move the ladders. Then we walked up to Rose and Stefano's house in town via Patigiani. Rose and Stefano shared the house with her cousin—they lived on the second floor and her cousin on the third. We walked upstairs and into the dining room. Rose opened the shutters to let the stream of sunlight fill the room. The dining room table could fit twenty people and was covered with three tablecloths. None of the cloths exactly matched, and none fit the entire length of the table. The table was set for the five of us. We sat down as directed by Rose. Sonya poured wine for everyone. Typically, we would drink water with a meal only after the first glass of wine, drinking it as plain water or as a wine-water mixture. For a moment, as I looked around the room, I thought of Uncle Nick and Aunt Lena, my father's sister and her husband. The table, chairs, juice glasses, and the aroma immediately took me back to my childhood. Stefano arrived with the tomatoes and mozzarella. He handed them to Rose, and off to the kitchen she went.

The small kitchen was off the dining room and overlooked the fields to the north of town. The room was small by American standards but certainly all that one needed to prepare an Italian feast. The dining room had the same stunning view of the fields. In a flash, Rose had the mozzarella cut and the tomatoes sliced. These would serve as my *secondo piatto* (meat course). The *primo piatto*, first course, was pasta. The pasta was always homemade—hand-kneaded and rolled. The tomato sauce was made from the fresh tomatoes in their garden. After we finished one very large bottle of Stefano's wine, a second was produced. *Mangiate*, eat, *bevette*, drink. After two courses, we had only just begun. There were two more courses—*formaggio* (cheese), *frutti* (fruit), next *dolce* (sweets), then grappa. It was now three in the afternoon. We were going back to work, but we had consumed a small cask of wine and now it was grappa time. I had to decline, but Rose insisted that if I was not going to drink the grappa, I must eat chocolate—and I did. It was now 3:30 p.m., and the church bells tolled. They rang to tell the town that lunch was over. Rose stood and cleared what was left on the table. She safely placed the leftovers in the oven.

I eventually became aware that Italians used their ovens as storage facilities. Remnants from the meal were placed in the oven for safekeeping. They would be consumed as part of the next meal. Rose collected the bottle of wine and some glasses, which she placed in a small cloth bag. For a moment, I was in disbelief, yet at the same time I thought I could acclimate to this lifestyle. I would become an Italian farmer!

We walked—more like stumbled—back to work. No one went up the *scala*—not just then. The most critical part of harvesting the olives is making sure that the *scala* is secure. Otherwise, one would find oneself hanging on to the ladder for dear life as it slipped and became perpendicular to the tree branches. The end result would be a direct descent to terra firma and your fellow harvesters. Because we were full of food, wine, grappa, and chocolate, we took our positions around the lower olive branches for now. After an hour, Stefano ventured on to *scala alto*. Soon, Rose joined him.

With all of our senses about us, conversation and laughter continued. Victor walked over from his grove to see if we were well and if lunch had been a success. We laughed and assured him it was *perfecto*. The sun was starting to set, and the last olive tree needed to be harvested—we couldn't leave a half-picked tree. This was an absolute. The pace picked up. The church bells tolled that it was five o'clock and the day's work done. We began gathering the *cassetti* full of olives, weighing what seemed like a ton each. We hobbled up the "Indian path," much like a line of ants with a picnic prize. We then collected the nets and ladders. Everything needed to be returned to the house; nothing was to be left in the grove. I'm not sure if there was fear that the wild boar at night might damage the nets or that the boars might, in fact, hold a Dionysian olive festival. Wild boars are known for their rogue night travels in the olive groves.

I thought this was the end of the day. I was prepared to drive to town to check into my hotel, but the day's work was not over. It was now time to *salute* to a day's work. The wine bottle Rose had brought from her house was opened, glasses were handed out, and we drank to a successful day and a successful tomorrow. I looked at the farmhouse and thought, *Someday you will be completely restored, and we will have lunch and drink our toast here.* The final *salute* was for a safe day's harvest tomorrow. We gathered up the glasses, nets, ladders. The *cassetti* were now safely stored for the evening, and it was time to venture home. I drove Rose and Stefano to their house. It had been a long day, and I knew they must be exhausted. *Ciao, e buona sera.* I looked around and realized how much I had learned and how willing this country and its people were to teach me.

I smell coffee and pastries. For a moment, I forget where I am. I drift back to today, although the senses evoked by my first harvest linger in my mind and soul. I look over at Mike. He seems to have drifted off during my harvest story, or maybe we both drifted off and it was all but a dream. I give him a gentle poke. It's time for him to wake up and get back to work.

"Should I report you to the proper agency for sleeping on the job?" I tease him.

"Did I snore?" he asks.

"No more than half the people on the plane, including me."

"Do you want to look out the window for a while?" he asks.

"No, it scares me. You can keep your window seats. I avoid them at all cost. I love to fly as long as I don't look out the window and realize just how high up we are." Breakfast is served.

"What are you doing when we land in Roma?" Mike asks.

"I will take the train up to Chiusi, but I have no specific

plans. Italians always say they have a plan, but they don't. Why do you ask?"

"I thought you might go to Roma for a couple of hours. I could check into my hotel at the airport, and we could ride the shuttle into Roma together."

"Why don't you check into your hotel and meet me in Roma at Termini," I suggest. "I'm not sure what the schedule is—I never know the schedule. Come to Termini. Usually, I have a two-hour window before my train leaves. But I must warn you, if there is a train at the station, I'll be on it."

"That sounds fair. I'll meet you at the station."

The plane makes its final approach to Roma, and it is time to gather our belongings. Mike pulls out a piece of paper and writes down his phone number.

"You know where my hotel is, if you have any problems."

"I can't imagine any problems, I will be fine."

The plane's wheels touch down, and the passengers in the rear of the plane begin clapping.

I think we have the smallest luggage on the plane."

Mike glances and says, "That's all you bring with you?"

"What do I need in the Italian countryside? It's not fashion week in Milano. Besides, I keep what I need here at the farm. The only problem I sometimes have is when I return to the States. The customs officer looks at me confused, as if wondering why I never purchase anything, why I have such a small bag, and why I am traveling alone."

Mike laughs and then says, "You know, we federal officials are always on the lookout for rogue traveling citizens like you."

With that we hug, promise to meet at the Termini station in two hours, and disembark.

"Can I cut the customs line with you?" I say, laughing at the thought.

"If only there were express lines to cut. *Baci e ciao.*"

Before we know it, we are out in the Italian air. Mike heads for the airport hotel, and I to the express train. The express train from Fiumicino Airport, the Leonardo Express, to Termini, the central train station of Roma, is approximately a thirty-minute journey. I purchase my ticket and wait for the next train to arrive. When it does, the scene reminds me of cattle being herded to a slaughterhouse. Hundreds of people line the platform, attempting to board the train, while at the same time; hundreds of other people attempt to disembark. It is a type of chaos every tourist should experience once in their life. It is not only that hundreds of people are bouncing into each other but that most are dragging large suitcases behind them. These large containers with their rolling wheels never seem to function properly, causing the owner to stop, jerk, and stumble the entire length of the platform. There always seems to be one broken wheel that causes the suitcase to tip over on its side. This, of course, causes a major traffic jam, as everyone attempts to steer clear of the disaster. This inevitably causes three more pile-ups.

I love the train ride from Termini to Chiusi. Normally, the train is half full and usually fifteen minutes late. Today is different—the train to Chiusi will leave in ten minutes. I purchase my ticket and board the train. *Oh my God,* I think in panic. *I forgot to validate my ticket.* I run off the train, looking for the little yellow box where everyone has to punch their ticket before boarding the train. I insert my ticket, hear the stamp sound, and run back to the train.

I watch the tourists and commuters as I board the train. I find a seat—though seats are often assigned, no one pays any heed—and then I hear the normal arrival and departure announcement. Tranitalia apologizes for being late. This is truly civil. I realize that no American train has ever apologized to me for being late. The train will leave around noon, so there is no question that everyone will eat lunch on the train. Out of small bags come large bottles of wine, along with fruit, meat, and cheese. I cannot believe the amount of food Italians take on the train with them. It is as if they fear they might be stranded for two months in the middle of nowhere with nothing to eat or drink.

Amazing, powerful aromas from the food and drink fill the train compartment, and the compartment becomes more a small version of an Italian kitchen. Because it is lunchtime, everyone engages in conversation. Though all are traveling strangers, a common topic of conversation is readily engaged. Today, as usual, it focuses on the latest transgression of the prime minister or president or the last great victory of the football team. It is at this point on my two-hour train ride that I finally realize I am home. The transition is finished, and it is hard for me to imagine I ever left. I think of Mike for a moment. He should be arriving at the Termini station. *I will call him later*, I tell myself.

I hear the faint sound of a bicycle bell, which means the small bicycle food cart—the refreshment cart—is coming down the aisle of the train compartment. The cart provides food and drink for those who have ill prepared themselves for the journey.

The train approaches the Chiusi station, but knowing which station is approaching takes practice, as there generally are no announcements—and if there are, they come just as the train pulls into the station, leaving little time for travelers to gather their belongings and disembark. The first few times I took the journey up to Chiusi, I noticed passengers getting up and gathering in the aisles. Only seasoned travelers know exactly where they are and that the next stop is their final destination. Practice makes train traveling in Italy easy.

The train pulls into Chiusi with its load of joyful passengers. I gather my one bag and disembark. The car rental agency is directly across from the train station. I have become friendly with the owners, and it always is a pleasure to see them again. Sarah and Sergio take turns running the office. They are wonderful and have the best rates in the entire Tuscany region. After we greet each other, Sarah fills me in on the local updates. We have an understanding—no big cars for Giovanna. I can't drive in small towns in Italy with a big car; I just can't fit through the streets of the walled cities. Somehow, though, I always manage to get a large car at least for a portion of my visit. Sarah tells me they will bring the large car over to the farm and pick up the small car. After three days, they will return the small car. It always happens, and we always laugh. I take the keys and say, "*Grazie*. Sarah. *Ciao*."

Chapter 3
Being

As I drive into Villastrada, I look over at the market. It's closed—I have forgotten about siesta. It usually takes me a couple of days to remember that the shops in Villastrada, with the exception of the café, close for three hours in the afternoon for siesta. I decide I'll drive over to Castiglione del Lago, which translates as Castle on the Lake, for lunch. The wind has picked up, and the lake should be beautiful, the perfect place for lunch. The drive over to Lago Trasimeno is through the countryside. This road does not have the sharp curves over rolling hills as does the road on the way to Chiusi. This road is straight and follows the railway lines. Large airplane-hangar–type buildings and red street stations line the road. It reminds me of old movies about World War II. I always expect to see a tank coming down the road with fighter planes overhead. Sometimes I can almost see the entire panoramic vista in black and white, as in the old movies, with the farmers out in the fields.

I drive through the small towns. The road is bustling this time of day. Everyone is returning home for lunch from the work in the fields. It is time to relax and enjoy the rewards of the morning's labor.

I arrive in Castiglione del Lago. The drive through lower Castiglione del Lago is a challenge only to those unfamiliar with

Italian walled cities. All walled cities have a reference point. The central *portone* always is designed by a black bull's-eye on a white sign. If the town names are referenced by *basso* (the newer and lower section), it is truly not the historic town you viewed in a Frommer's travel guide. The term "lower" means the most recent addition just outside of the walled city. Most were constructed after World War II. The architecture of the lower portions of many towns has what I call the "1950s Miami, Florida, look." The original town was built sometime between AD 700 and 1500. The juxtaposition of the ancient with the hurried, later construction of housing and shelter is startling at first. It is also a painful reminder of the casualties of war—lost lives and cities. The drive between home and this small lake town is living history for me. Driving to any walled city generally causes me to ask myself, "Can my car fit through the *portone*, and will I ever find a parking spot?"

I drive down the hill and arrive at Lago Trasimeno. The wind is now blowing almost at gale force; the lake is rolling into large whitecaps. The wind and water appear as if in competition as to which might be the mightier—or maybe each wishes to share a part with the other, one showing the strength of the other. The wind rushes across the water's surface, and the water is forced to resist. Today, whitecaps and wind are the interplay of nature's elements.

I park along the lake and walk into the restaurant. It has a perfect view of the lake. The sounds of Italy are the sounds of voices. The baritone voice of the owner meets the soprano voice of a child. Groups of people smile and talk; their hands are the batons of conductors. The symphony in the restaurant is conducted by one man, Anthony. He and his wife are serving the entire dining room. There is time for a long lunch, usually two and a half hours. Outside, the wind now moves the leaves and branches of the large trees surrounding the lake. Their shadows are cast on the stucco walls, and a dance is added to the symphony. A ballet of nature and humans now surrounds my view and thoughts. Ah, another story of Italy—Italy has many stories to tell from within and without. For those who are taken under the wing of this land, there is no explanation, a spiritual understanding. Whitecaps, branches, voices, wind, clouds, and hands—the ballet is in place. The church bells from upper Castiglione del Lago ring out over the sound of the wind that forces itself through the leaves.

I sit down and drift back to my Italy—the Italy in which I grew up; specifically, the aroma from the kitchen. The voices begin to call me back. ...

It was early on a Sunday. A voice called from downstairs— more akin to a bell than a voice, and it always called three times. It was time to wake. There was no sleeping late on Sunday. It would take time for everyone to put themselves together. The garter belts, the stockings, Sunday's best dress, the search for the lost Sunday shoes and discovery of yet another hiding place—once our Sunday uniforms were in place, it was time to accessorize with Sunday missal, veil, and gloves. What about the rosary beads? A quick look in the mirror prevented Mom's licked finger from attempting to contain any wandering hair.

Everyone in the family was ready; it was time to get into the family car. If anyone was missing any of the above items, a small family feud would ensue. This ritual always played at 9 a.m. on Sunday at our house. Breakfast would wait until later. As Catholics, we didn't eat breakfast before receiving the host—the body of Christ. There was no deviation to this "law." Money for collection was handed out in the car. The church car was the new Mercury paneled station wagon with a back seat and a "back-back" seat. Mom drove with Dad in the front and the four children in the back. Age dictated seating position. The old gray Packard was for everyday driving.

My father was Italian; his family's first language was Italian. In our house, everyone went to church—there was not an option. We followed the same procedure every Sunday: we would park down the road (always on the right side) and walk up to the church as a family unit. Dad would open the door, and Mom would go in, followed by the children.

The procession walked down to the front pew—this was not to be missed. Again, age dictated position. Mother was in the lead, with the children still following—genuflect, holy water, proceed down the aisle. If there was a deviation in the procedure, it was due to sibling rivalry, which then resulted in one child's being placed on the left side of the matriarch—a display to the world (and more importantly, to God) of disobedience. Mom did not hesitate to exercise this power.

Mass begins, then spoken in Latin. The words: *Santa Rose, anno domino,* and *I noma di pace.* Dad, known to all as Jake, always stood at the back of the church. He was an usher and always wore the same suit. He had one suit—it was all he needed. The suit was pale blue, purchased by my English mother—"Dad's uniform," we would call it. My dad was a simple man—one comb, one toothbrush, and his set of work clothes consisting of khaki pants and shirts. Dad was what I call "Italian short, the normal height for an Italian, a short man by American standards,." He had thick, black wavy hair, which later in life turned pure white. It was beautiful. When he was younger, he was in great shape but later developed the Italian "waist-widening," as I call it, put another way as he aged he became shorter and wider. He had a heart of gold. If people needed something he had, he would gladly give it to them. He was number six out of nine children. When he was fourteen, his father died. At the time, he was the second eldest living at home with his mother. So Dad and his brother Augie took on the responsibilities of provider and protector.

Their father had supported the family by working as a brickyard foreman. All the sons worked at the brickyard at one point or another. But in 1927, Augie and Jake started a new adventure. They left the brickyard behind and opened up their own businesses on the Island. Augie ran a garage; Dad ran a marina, coal yard, and gas station. They worked hard and played hard. Their life and times became an island legacy. Before there were commercial banks on the island, Dad was known to all as the local "bank." To this day, people refer to a large pile of money as "a Jake wad."

I smile to myself.

My thoughts are broken by Antonio, the "conductor" of the restaurant. He informs me of the daily specials and makes suggestions—he never fails the diner. The restaurant is full of life—children, parents, grandparents. Everyone is together, enjoying the moment and life together. Yes, this is humanity at its best. Time has no presence; here is only the heartbeat of life. I order water, wine, and the house pasta of the day.

The wind and water are still antagonizing each other. I gaze out the window and smile. My soul affords me this liberty of peace and family. My water and wine arrive. I thank God and the universe and salute to life. The smells of freshness and the earth fill the dining room. A small boy, sitting with his mother and her friend, smiles at me. He has made friends with everyone in the dining room. Children are considered a gift in Italy. Maybe it is because so many children, women, and men have lost their lives. For thousands of years, wars were fought on their soil. This also may explain three observations I have had here: the love of life, the importance of family, and the richness of the soil. The richness of the soil I believe is from the blood of those who lost their lives. The redemption of that loss is the beauty and nourishment the land now provides. Tragedy is transformed into a peaceful, bountiful countryside. *Pace* (peace) is everywhere in Italy. You see it when you walk down the streets of towns, in the fields, and in the eyes of men and women who lived through the last world war.

The loss of seventeen Italian soldiers in the Iraq war brought the people of Italy together to mourn. A million strong lined the streets of Roma. The city closed its shops in horror and honor to the sons of this country. The people of Italy would not allow this atrocity to continue. Italy withdrew its soldiers from the conflict. All was at *pace,* (peace). Every November, each town lays a wreath at its war memorial to remember this last painful conflict.

I go back to my thoughts of church as a child—Sunday, Communion, and the second collection.

Dad was the usher on the left side of the church. The family always sat on the left side. During collection time, Dad always was serious and yet placed the offering basket in front of each of us with a gentle smile. Like an orchestrated movement, each of us placed the offering in the green felt-lined basket. There existed a rule regarding the amount of money placed in the basket for each offering. The first offering was always change: fifty cents for adults and a dime for the children. The stakes for the second offering were raised: adults—one dollar; children—a quarter. How this was established may have specifically been my father's interpretation of what we, as a unit, were able to provide. For me, the second collection was a benchmark—it meant mass was about to end. The body and blood of Christ were in you, communion was over and the offering for this service appropriately made, and most important part--"go in peace." Although mass was officially over, it was not yet over for me until Father Garvey led his sheep out of the church. His journey to the back of the church and his procession was deserving of the Pope. I wondered on this Sunday why Father Garvey was taking so long to walk down the aisle. He was old, but old people had the ability to walk at a proper pace. His ending his all-important weekly ritual, however, did not amount to his running down the aisle. Paramount to him was keeping his sheep a few moments longer in the hope of some salvation and reflection.

Once we finally are outside the church, the fresh air replaced the years of incense and flowers. The smell of incense lingered eternally inside the church. Every incense offering, whether for the celebration of birth, communion, confirmation, marriage, or death, continually lingered in the air. The smell of lilies never seemed to leave, and the combined odors created a sacred scent. The years of prayer and song were encased in this interior. The sun was bright, and the darkness of the church quickly was forgotten, as well the message of the Mass. The hour of kneeling, standing, sitting, and singing was over. For small children, that hour was an eternity. (And as far as the church was concerned, that thought could cost me an eternity in hell.) We all ran to the car. There no longer was the need for order and presentation. Now the mission was to get into the car and go. We hoped it would not take Dad long to finish his usher duties and that Mom would not linger, talking to the members of the choir. This after-Mass socializing was an important ritual that could not be overlooked.

When everyone was in the car, the first stop was the gas station. The gas station was one of the businesses my father and Uncle Augie started in 1927. It is the oldest family-owned Mobil gas station and marina in America—a proud testament to my father's dedication to work, family, and life.

Dad had to check on things. We remained in the car, our veils off and prayer books in a pile, patiently waiting for Dad's return. When we got home, we sprang out of the car and ran into the house. All the accessories of mass immediately were stowed. The line for the bathroom was formed. Mother's mandatory rule: everyone has to go to the bathroom before the rest of the day can begin. Mother's rules were not to be broken; Dad had no rules.

Sunday-best–dressed children then climbed back into the paneled wagon. The best part of Sunday was about to begin. The ferry boat was the next hurdle. If we missed the scheduled boat or if it was full, it would be half an hour before the ferry returned to take us to the mainland.

In my mind, we were basically going home—"home" in the sense that we were going to my father's family home to be with his brothers, sisters, and a pod of their children. We would be all together, all living life. Our arrival was incredible. The car doors flew open at once, and we dashed to the door. Aunt Lena seemed to have a sixth sense and knew exactly the moment the car pulled up. She would be standing with the door open and a gentle smile on her face. The greeting process was simple: everyone had to pinch everyone's cheeks twice. This process could take up to ten minutes, depending on the exact number of individuals already at Uncle Nick and Aunt Lena's. Uncle Nick and Aunt Lena cooked all morning, and I always silently asked myself, *Didn't they have to go to Mass?* The aromas of their morning labors filled the air both inside and outside their home.

Aunt Mary lived in an attached apartment. Her husband died years before I was born, and her two sons had grown, married, and moved off to start their own businesses. Aunt Mary always seemed to have stillness about her. While all the other aunts and uncles would toss their hands, speak loudly, laugh, and curse in Italian, Aunt Mary had a very quiet side. She was a pensive woman with a small Italian physique. She always wore black—I don't think she ever recovered from the loss of her beloved husband.

Aunt Lena and Uncle Nick married very young—she was fourteen and he sixteen years old. The two cornerstones of their living room were their wedding photograph and a large oil painting of Saint Marco's Square in Venice. The room was always "Italian dark" and never changed—it looked the same, it smelled the same, and it would always be Aunt Lena and Uncle Nick's. Remembering them always makes a smile come to my face. In their home, their music was Italia—the music created of voices and life. They did not have a Victrola; they had their voices; and as with most Italian families, they had an accordion that everyone played. This group of Italians loved nothing more than a good "O Solo Mio," and it never seemed to matter to anyone if the musical key or the words were right. To them, anything and everything that was fun was right, and when more members joined in, more fun was guaranteed.

I hear, "*Prego*." I look up, and Antonio is standing by my table. My pasta has arrived, and of course, a little more water and wine will complete the entree. The wind and water finally have called a truce. The white caps have turned into gentle, rolling waves, and the seabirds return to flight. It is a perfect spring day. The symphony of voices, with hands conducting, continues. There is beauty and love here, but most important, there are the vibrancies of life. It is time to be grateful, to be thankful, and to enjoy the gifts that have been shared. ...

In Lena and Nick's kitchen, the pots on the stove were large enough that I could have climbed inside. Aunt Lena had an enormous scar on her upper left arm. Apparently, when she was a small child, she was helping her mother make pasta, and the boiling water scalded her. When asked about it, she smiled and said, "Oh, that old thing." Her round face never showed signs of wrinkles; her eyes were knowing and kind. She wore a hairnet over her silvery-gray hair, which was short and curled. She was short with a soft roundness. She and Uncle Nick were animated with their loud voices and waving of arms. Their personalities were melodic, resembling a modern jazz improv. The aroma of handmade pasta, sausage, sauces, and fish filled the air—those scents would never leave my memory. The table was as long as the room, and every chair the neighborhood had to offer was brought into the kitchen. Nothing matched in their kitchen, yet everything was perfect. Jelly jars doubled as drinking glasses for the children.

After everyone arrived and was greeted properly, the first order of the day was eating and drinking. The food always appeared to be piled as high as Mount Etna. Milk did not exist at our table—children drank wine mixed with water. When the feasting was over but not the drinking, we would seek haven outside if the weather permitted. The side yard was incredibly small but was filled with beautiful vegetable plants. We sat under the grape arbor, which had been planted by Uncle Nick. In season, the arbor was laden with grapes, and the scent was intoxicating. The table wine served during any meal was always from this arbor. A few cousins attempted to plant and grow grapes, hoping the end result would be wine, but it was just hoping on their part, and it was a total failure. In fact, one cousin's wine was so bad, it would have been better to put it on salad.

Italian always was spoken during the family meals, and this drove my mother crazy—*pazzo, pazzo*—so crazy, in fact, that she banned everyone from speaking Italian in "her" house. Apparently, it was the result of my grandmother's calling my mother *pazzo* that led to the discontinuation of the Italian language in our home.

The families were all from the same small town, Popoli, in Italy. Oral histories of family members who remained in Italy were told. The river running through Popoli was always a favorite topic for Uncle Nick. He and Aunt Lena first met in a small eastern Long Island town, were married, and created their version of Popoli in their backyard. The laughter, drinking, and eating of cheese and fruit continued until the sun was about to set. By this time, the children were piled high on the sofa, along with pocketbooks, sweaters, and coats. The challenge of matching child with handbag and family was always the closing event of the day.

I am brought back to the present by a little boy in the restaurant. He runs to each table, smiling and asking everyone's name. Climbing up on the chair, he smiles and proceeds to inform everyone in the restaurant of his day's activities. There are no strangers here. It's easy to drift back while sitting here. It is familiar and comfortable. The restaurant has nothing made of paper. Everything is cloth—nothing fancy, just Italian cloth. I'll have more wine and water and finish my pasta.

The diners come and go, but tables are left cluttered. Apparently, there is no urgency to remove what is a memory of a great meal. My pasta, served in a spicy tomato sauce, is fantastic—*perfecto*. I finish the last bite. Antonio comes to the table to inquire about *dolce*—dessert. How can I pass up dessert on a Saturday afternoon while overlooking the lake? Impossible.

Antonio presents my options, and I choose tiramisu. He smiles. "A perfect choice," he assures me. Soon, Antonio's wife, Gina, arrives and smiles her gentle smile.

I tell her, "The pasta was perfect."

She thanks me and walks back into the kitchen. I take a bite of tiramisu and look out at the lake. My eyes fill with tears. That lake that danced with the wind is now a pool of my tears. Each tear falls slowly, Rinny...the queen of tiramisu. Rinny made the best tiramisu in the world. She made pans of it, and she could devour a whole pan by herself. I think of Lena and Rinny. They both could make magic in the kitchen, though they never met each other. Aunt Lena passed away just before Rinny was born. As Rinny grew, her love for life and cooking would remind me of Lena. She shared the same physical stature, but it was truly their love for laughter, cooking, and life that married them together. They each had a need to make sure everyone was taken care of, well fed, and well protected. Now, they are both gone—cooking the family Sunday lunch for everyone in heaven. I imagine everyone who was sitting at Uncle Nick and Aunt Lena's Sunday kitchen table is together, and they are now with my Rinny, and the table is filled with laughter and the spirit of kindness. Eventually, we will all end up around their kitchen table.

I realized at the time of Rinny's birth that naming her Lenora would be more of a prophecy than an endearing wish to remember my aunt. Rinny honored Lena's memory and name. I thought of Rinny's choice of names when it was time for her confirmation. While most of the children in confirmation class took the classic saints' names, like John, Anthony, Rose, and Paul, Rinny chose Atlantis and never once explained her decision to anyone. I often wonder how the priest allowed such a choice. Atlantis was a lost pagan city. In what manner did that name fit into the doctrine of the Catholic Church? Rinny had a magical aura and certainly a convincing ability unmatched by many. In hindsight, God didn't seem to mind. If my dream could be answered, I would be sitting here with Aunt Lena and Rinny, sharing the latest kitchen adventure.

I remember the story Uncle Nick told us on many Sundays—the trials of Aunt Lena's attempting to learn to drive. This story was always told well after lunch was finished, and we were sitting under the grape arbor, which was next to the garage. The story goes like this:

Nick stood outside the car, directing Lena into the garage. He said, "Lena, step on the gas." As Aunt Lena drove into the garage, Nick failed to tell her to step on the brake, so Lena drove through the garage. Nick, beside himself, yelled, "Lena, step on the brake!" Lena complied. Uncle Nick then screamed at her go in reverse. Aunt Lena placed the car in reverse and proceeded out of the garage, across the street, and into the neighbor's shrubs. From all accounts, that was the last time Lena ever drove.

Whenever Uncle Nick told this story, filling the group with laughter, Lena's response was, "I got in the garage. If you had closed the door when I backed out, the door would have stopped me, and I would not have rolled into the neighbor's shrubs." At this, Uncle Nick always raised his hands high in frustration.

I had a similar experience while teaching Rinny to drive. We lived in New Hampshire at the time, just off a rather busy four-lane street. We had a manual transmission car, and Rinny was out for an afternoon practice drive. All was going well, when Rinny had to stop to make the left-hand turn. Just as she is making her turn, the car lurched forward and stalled. Rinny, without a care in the world, looked at me and laughed. A gentleman passing in his car stopped to see if everything was all right. Rinny responded, "Just learning to drive." It took at least two minutes for her to get herself back together and moving forward.

Tears run down my face now. Outside, I see the wind and

water have taken on their singular identities. The tiramisu sits in front of me. Rinny's laugh and Lena's smile come to me again. Tiramisu has been a staple family dessert. My siblings and I always attempted to out-eat the other. A tray of tiramisu the size of a lasagna pan would be placed on the table, and away we'd go. *It's amazing that the entire family didn't turn into an advertisement for Weight Watchers*, I reflect. Now, I finish the bittersweet dessert. This was the end of a meal and of a life. My thoughts return me to my childhood Sunday lunch. ...

We children all were safely piled back in our cars, each child and handbag returned to the proper family. We were sleepy from food and the small sips of wine. It didn't matter now whether the ferry returned immediately. Time seemed of little importance. Our Sunday—the day we looked forward to every week—was over. Tomorrow would bring school and the tolling of the three bells—those being my mother's voice.

I hear Antonio's voice off in the distance and return to my lunch at the lake.

As I finish my wine and look out at the lake, the family I am sitting next to becomes my family. There is no sense of urgency. Time becomes life; urgency will make you old and cranky. Italy has no place for old and cranky. To be old, you must be over two thousand years old. To be cranky means you are not alive. Antonio comes over to my table to inquire whether everything was satisfactory, which of course it was. We smile. And he brings my coffee. Coffee always is served after *dolce*, never with it. There is serenity outside. For a moment, the outside world becomes a classic still life. The shadows of leaves on the stucco building form into the shapes of statues, the movements of their earlier ballet now frozen, as if a photograph, by the stillness of the air.

Il conto—the bill. I regret the thought of having to leave, but the restaurant has emptied, and the day must move on. I pay and then kiss Antonio and his wife, thanking them for their kindness. I walk out to the lake.

Chapter 4
Learning

I walk along the lakeshore and look over to the islands. There are three islands in Lago Trasimeno. Isola Maggione, the second largest island, is where St. Francis spent Lent. The story is that he was rowed out on Fat Tuesday with two loaves of bread for the entire six weeks of Lent. When the fisherman rowed back to meet him to return him to town, St. Francis still had one and a half loaves of bread with him. Today, there is a small village on the island. On the island are the ruins of an early Franciscan monastery from the 14th century. The women of the *isola,* (island) are known for their beautiful lace work, which is prized by all of Italy. The largest Isola Polvese is a national park preserve; the third is Minore, it is now uninhabited.

Fishermen now journey out on the lake, setting and pulling in their nets, providing the area with fresh local *pesce* (fish). The small white ferry moves gracefully through the becalmed water. It carries its passengers to the small island and across the lake to the small towns that dot its shores. Siesta will continue. I sit down on a bench and look out, as life is truly lived. The families from the restaurant are enjoying the lakeshore. The children run and laugh, dogs wag tails, and the world is at peace. A small child runs up to me and smiles, touches my hand, laughs, and runs down to the shore. The world is as the world should be—a safe haven for all. There are no fears. Gentle kindness embraces us all.

Two sailboats approach from the east. They are sailing downwind, their white sails pure and full. The color of the sky is an ocean blue and it's filled with clouds only the heavens could make. I'll stay a moment longer—the wind and water are my elements, providing me with life and love. The land provides me with a base for my soul to touch reality, if I am close and wise enough to listen. I smile. The church bells up in the town ring sounds of joy. What once was a lake of my tears is now an ocean of my joys and life's gifts.

I am taken back to childhood again. ...

When we were little, we would go crabbing or fishing. In the morning, we made sandwiches and walked down to the creek. We had a small wooden dory that provided the transportation for our crabbing expeditions. Uncle Nick loved it when we went crabbing. A bushel of fresh crabs was something my mother hated but something every Italian loved.

We spent the morning on the creek, crabbing and having our lunch. When the bushel was full, we returned home, to the smiles of Uncle Nick. It was apparent to us that the only days to crab were the days when Uncle Nick visited. He would take our harvest home to Lena, Eddie, and Mary for their evening meal. One day we returned from crabbing and left the bushel of crabs outside the house under the grape arbor that Uncle Nick had made for us. Off we went on another childhood adventure, knowing Uncle Nick would take the churning bushel of crabs home. Somewhere between the time we left the crabs and Uncle Nick was to take them, the family dog found them. Duchess, the well-loved mixed-breed family dog, knocked the bushel over, just to play with them. A bushel of crabs running around the front door of the house—what a joy for a playful dog! But at that moment, Mom appeared. As I've said, Mom was no fan of anything from the sea, least of all things with legs. One look at the scurrying creatures was all it took to set her off. She jumped in the car and drove down the hill; she would find Nick and Jake. I'm not sure what transpired at that juncture, but from that day on, we were forbidden to ever bring a crab near the house. Any we caught had to be left down the hill at the gas station. There were no questions asked; thy mother's will be done. That night, Mom burned some chicken to show her dissatisfaction with the day's events.

I look out at the lake and reflect on my first time enjoying her shores. I had purchased the farm and, as all land purchases in Italy go, the process actually was the joy. A purchase in Italy is like a deal between buyer, seller, agent, God, and the devil. I say that with great respect. I wanted to return to the roots of my father's family and the Italian childhood joys for which I longed. My soul was driving me home, but at the time, I did not understand. I was led to the Tuscan/Umbria border. I knew where my heart and soul were; now I needed a place for my physical body. Upon returning home to America, I searched the Internet and found an agent. My list of must-haves was long, but the list of properties was short. After a few months, eight potential properties appeared. It was time to take the journey to Italy and be safely home with my soul and memories. ...

The first house I went to look at was Olivetta. I fell in love. My heart, soul, and being said, "This is your home." The agent informed me that the property had been on and off the market because any offer accepted was later refused. Saddened, I returned to my hotel. The next day I received a call from the agent, informing me that the owners, Mario and Gina, wanted to meet with me at their home. We met, and I explained in my limited Italian that my family was from Popoli on the eastern coast of Italy. I said I would be grateful if they would sell Olivetta to me. Before giving me an answer, we agreed that I would have lunch at their home.

I arrived and parked outside their large country house, which overlooked Olivetta, my new dream. I rang the doorbell, and Gina greeted me with the standard two kisses and the informal greeting *"Com e sta?"* The house was the traditional Italian farmhouse style. The entire ground floor was empty; presumably, if the need to have farm animals should arise, they easily would be accommodated. We walked upstairs into an enormous living room. This was my first encounter with an Italian country home. There was no clutter and no electronics, but there was a profusion of photographs from every generation, each in a place of honor. Mario was wearing what I, as a child, *thought* was the Italian male "uniform"—button-up vest, tie, and trousers. The crucifix and the picture of the Pope all reminded me of my childhood. I was home. The aromas from the *cucina* made me smile. *Aunt Lena and Uncle Nick must be cooking inside*, I thought wistfully. Gina's kitchen was small, consisting of a stove, sink, table, and a small window. On the table sat a bottle of homemade wine, a bottle of water, and a loaf of today's bread, wrapped in paper. We sat down to wine first. What amazed me was the lack of kitchen countertop clutter—no toaster, coffeemaker, blender, TV, radio, pile of mail, or other American-type countertop debris. We talked; I wanted to know about Mario and Gina, their lives, and their family and history.

Gina informed me that their children were grown, each married with children and a farm of their own. Gina and Mario had decided it was time to sell Olivetta, as they could not work the farm any longer, and the house was in need of repair. It was a difficult decision. A major chapter in their life was about to close. We laughed; the stories of life were stories of joy. Like every true Italian who invites you in to dine, Gina was concerned that I was not eating enough. I assured her that I had plenty to eat. When the *secondo platto*—meat—arrived, I took a breath and explained I did not eat meat. Gina looked at me with alarm. She asked, "Does your father know you don't eat meat?"

Doing all I could to keep from breaking into a full belly laugh, I responded, "Yes, though he used to think it was a single-meal event and that I would eat meat at the next meal. After

fifteen years, he proudly said, 'Giovanna does not eat meat.'"
Gina, put her hands to her cheeks and smiled.

We talked about the town and about World War II—the
horrors and what happened to the women, children, and men of
this small town. It was hard for Gina to talk about these events.
I understood. Olivetta, she told me, had been "restored" after
damage from that war. She added proudly, "Olivetta is a good
and solid house."

I thought, *What does she mean by restored?* The portion of
the wall destroyed during the war had been repaired, but they
had not lived in the house for thirty years. In fact, the condition
of the "restored" house with which I had fallen in love was as
follows: the lower level was home to animals. Long feeding
troughs filled the large rooms. The second floor had the living
quarters, which included an enormous fireplace in which to cook
and a small seat to climb on to warm oneself during cold nights.
The plumbing in the house was limited to a sink. Electricity
consisted of two light bulbs hanging from the ceiling in the
bedroom and "kitchen." The house was amazingly clean; Gina
tended to it weekly. I assured them I loved the house. I planned
to turn the original pigsties on the first floor into living space,
and the newer pigsties constructed at the side of the house, in
the late 1950s would be renovated.

We lingered. Gina made coffee as a sign the meal was over.
She told more stories and her round face and reddish/black
Italian hair reminded me of why I was in Italy, why my soul
needed a home and an Italian family. We finished, and again I
offered to help with the cleanup, but Gina would have nothing
to do with that. I thanked them again and pleaded with them to
consider my purchase of their Olivetta. I kissed Mario *buona
sera*. Gina walked me down to the front door. We kissed, and
she smiled and put both of her hands on my checks. Anyone
who is Italian knows that this is a sign of blessing, acceptance,
understanding, and anything that is good in life. I went back to
the hotel to await the verdict. Before long, my phone rang. Mario

and Gina had agreed to sell at the price I'd offered. *Grazie*, I thought. I asked the agent to assure them I would love Olivetta and become a productive Italian farmer.

What I didn't truly understand was the "becomes an Italian farmer" part. It took two months to fill in all the documents, with thirteen trips to the consortium and five trips to find the right tax stamp at the local tobacco store. This finally happened, however, with the help of a small army of locals and friends who walked me through it, step by step. Although the steps continually change each year for no apparent reason, I now carry my annual official PAC card, Politic Agricola Comune, with pride, making sure never to miss the annual renewal.

Somewhere in the back of my mind, perhaps telepathically, I hear Rose calling, "Giovanna." Yes, it is time to go. The church bells have rung four o'clock. I am late. Rose will understand. I'll stop at the nursery and pick up more soil to replant the lavender and rosemary. Rose will be proud that I've remembered, and we can commence work when I return, though I'm sure she and Stefano will have rekindled half of the cut olive branches in the grove, and I will see the smoke from many kilometers away on the drive home. Still sleepy from the food, wine, and afternoon's delights, I walk to the car and begin my journey back to Olivetta.

I decide to stop for an espresso at the café in town. It should give me enough energy to keep me alert for the late-afternoon farm activities. The men of the town have gathered to share their thoughts before returning to their afternoon labors. This resembles the morning social gathering but has become a midday news update. Certainly, this is the first opportunity they have had to gather since their morning cappuccino. The updates are on family, fields, and the afternoon's plans. It took a while for me to acclimate to the long lunches, late starts, and evening schedule. Now I am uncertain as to how anyone could live any other way. Dinner is long off. I drive to the market for bread, cheese, wine. The market is a hub of earthy freshness. Every item comes from the local farmers, and although I am a vegetarian, I am impressed with the quality of the meats and the variety of soppressatas, capicols, sausages and various species. Yes, I mean species, as here you will find every possible animal of the forest and the farmers' backyards. Sometimes I'm sure the rabbits and chickens on display are the ones from my neighbor's backyard. I smile at the thought and again think of Uncle Nick and the "mysterious vanishing family pets."

Roberto and his family are the local owners of the market, as well as owning a great deal of the surrounding farmland and a large *agriturismo*, an Italian-style country bed-and-breakfast. He is also here behind the meat counter, greeting everyone and always seeming to ask just the right question and provide the perfect words of advice. He comes out from behind the counter, butcher apron shining bright crimson, covered with the labors of his morning. We kiss, laugh, and talk about this year's crops and the spring pruning of the olive trees. The beauty is that life is important enough to stop what you're doing and properly enjoy a reunion with a friend. Not only is the market a hub of freshness, but it has everything and anything anyone might need to survive. You need wine; they have it. You need fireplace starter; they have it. You need a toothbrush, hair coloring, frying pan, candle for the cemetery—they have it all. They always have it. My favorite sight is the Brunello wine placed next to the cookies. How can you have wine without cookies? Chocolate is a short distance off. Before I leave, Roberto's father asks, as always, "Do you want to sell some farmland?"

I smile. "Not this year."

It is a short drive to the garden nursery in town, which, in fact, is more like a hardware store, nursery, and farm equipment supplier. The owners are Gina and Mario's children. It is always a pleasure to stop in and make my purchases here. We talk of how the land was worked when they were children and what changes have occurred. We realize there has been little change to the lifestyle of this town and its inhabitants. I explain I need soil for planting the herbs I have purchased. They advise me on which works best and how I should plant the lavender and rosemary. In the back of my mind, I am certain I hear Rose calling, "Giovanna," not once but three times. I also say to myself, *I hope this is the way Rose thinks the lavender and rosemary should be planted*. Rose is tough—and not just a little tough. She will stand her ground like a fighting pit bull if she thinks you have strayed from her wisdom and advice. I've seen it firsthand. I thank the owners for their time. *Ciao e baci*, (goodbye and kisses). I am on my way to Olivetta.

Rose and Stefano obviously have been diligently working in the fields. The clouds of smoke coming from the olive grove are a testament to that. The smell of burning olive branches is distinct—a signature of the Umbria/Tuscany countryside during spring and again in the fall, when the olives are harvested and the branches pruned. I cannot help but be grateful for the use and care of this land. Driving by the "village dump"—a small Dumpster—smile to myself. How can a town survive with such a small receptacle for waste? It's simple; there is no waste—no over-packaging, no plastic to-go cups, no plastic bags. Actually, plastic bags are available, but you must buy them. This is the incentive to bring your own bag with you when shopping. (Italy, I thank you for your wisdom and ability to avoid the worst of consumerism.) I drive down the dirt driveway to the farmhouse. Victor is working in his grove. I see Rose and Stefano, hard at work in the far section of my grove.

I park the car, gather my belongings, and fumble for the house key. When I open the door, the scent of the farmhouse catches me off guard. It has been three months since I have been home. There is a distinct odor to a country farmhouse, a combination of earth and fire. It is truly spellbinding.

I open the doors and windows. The breezes fill the house, and the ever-present smell of burning olive branches fills the room. Rose is just walking up from the grove, and we greet each other with *Ciao e baci*, (Hello and kisses). I tell her that my plane was late so I went to Castiglione del Lago for lunch and on the way back, I picked up some soil and plants for the garden. She smiles with approval. She then, as always, raises her two hands to the side of her face, a true Italian sign of "well done."

As a surprise, Rose and Stefano have purchased fruit trees for me, and now Rose points to them—apple, pear, fig, and peach. According to Rose, an Italian farmhouse needs to have fruit trees. Olivetta soon will be returned to a true Umbrian working farm. Smiling and laughing, I hug her. Stefano comes up from the fields and the celebration continues briefly. They will plant the trees for me; the potting soil I just purchased will help the trees to be *forte* (strong). With this said, I understand that Rose will confiscate my potting soil (this is the side of Rose that at times can test my patience), so I'd best go buy some more if I plan to plant my lavender and herbs.

I quickly change into my Italian work uniform—a green overall jumpsuit, and am ready for my orders from Rose. She is in the field with Stefano, so I begin clearing the rocks and the debris left behind by the renovation. I remember Rose's persistent advice that certain items, such as bricks, pieces of stone, and wire, should be saved. Everything here is saved. A discarded piece of wire will hold the *cassetti* together when we store them in the fall after the olive harvest. A brick can be reused for a plethora of things. I begin the rock-sorting process and while doing so, I notice that my neighbor has taken an old door from my pigsty and incorporated it into his newly constructed multispecies pavilion for his chickens, goats, rabbits, and ducks. I laugh at the brilliant orange door; it cannot be missed.

"Good for him," I say to myself. The Italian countryside rule, apparently, is if it sits in your yard for more than three years, it is public property. Any item will be used where and when it's best suited. I wonder if he will offer me a few eggs one day as a sign of gratitude.

Rose now directs me to move the broken pieces of stone and rock to the driveway. *Recycle! Recycle* is her battle cry.

"The debris will help build up the driveway and keep the dust down"—simply stated and simply Rose. The "Law of Rose" always must be obeyed.

While I work with a plastic pail, which is really an old paint bucket that I am sure has served four lifetimes of functions, Victor, my neighbor, walks up from his olive grove. His farm is a second home—an alternative lifestyle from his urban lifestyle in Perugia.

"Giovanna, can I help?" he calls out.

I raise my hands to my checks and make the motion of prayer, adding "Santa Maria."

Victor looks like he is either Ralph Lauren or someone out of Lauren advertisements. His whitish-gray hair is full with the signature gentle Italian wave. His smile is captivating. He is wearing his typical Italian harvesting uniform. The uniform is a tattered, old sweater and worn blue jeans. Victor is the town translator, at least between Stefano, Rose, and me. I speak a little Italian and a little French, as my native language is English; Victor speaks a little English and French as a native Italian. Our conversations are an animated comedy. Sometimes I think my neighbors believe they are watching an old black-and-white cartoon. Whatever words neither of us can speak in Italian or English are spoken in French. I always carry a dictionary with me. Construction terms in Italian are the only portion of the language that is easy for me, as I was forced to learn them as I restored the house. Though the first contractor spoke English, he certainly had his own interpretation of my wishes and the English language (hence, the description of him as "the first contractor").

I walk down to meet Victor, and we walk up the narrow path together to the house, which is filled with the late afternoon sun. We sit down at one of Italy's most beautiful farm tables to discuss the events since my last time here. Stefano and Rose have returned from the olive grove and stop briefly to chat with us. I ask if they would like to join us for a glass of wine.

They gracefully decline, as they must continue with their work. Rose glances at me and smiles. I have passed Italian Hospitality 101.

Victor and I are now alone. I pour a glass of wine for each of us and ask if he might help me with a personal quest. "I learned of a local farmer named Carlo through an article in the *New York Times*. I'm trying to locate him and the professor at the University of Perugia who is working with him to preserve his heirloom seeds." I know Victor has connections with the University of Perugia and might be of help.

"I don't know the professor," he informs me. "Locating the local farmer might be simpler."

"The farmer's family has used only their own dried seeds for generations, literally hundreds of years," I explain. These precious seeds produce tomatoes, legumes, and Trasimeno beans. The tomatoes are self-preserving and will remain fresh after harvest, well through the winter, and the beans and legumes seem to be extremely resistant to any type of blight. Victor is intrigued and questions me about these seeds. I find it easier to produce the article and allow him to peruse it slowly for any information I have not clearly provided. We talk, we drink, and we laugh. Victor suggests that we walk to his house to look through the local phone book for Carlo's phone number or address.

I look at Victor in amazement, "There is a phone book for this area?"

His response is laugher. "*Si*, we are small, but we have phone books. That is how we can call each other."

I look confused. "I have seen very few phones here in the countryside. Are you sure?" Victor could barely contain his laughter. "The people I know only have cell phones."

Victor laughs again. "*Si*, but a few of us do have phones, and we need to have a phone book."

We walk up the driveway to Victor's house and enter into the *primo piano* (first floor). There is an entire one-man wine-processing plant here. I am amazed to see such a production center in the "basement" of his house. I tell him I would love to learn and help next time he begins the winemaking process. There is absolutely nothing automated or industrialized in his process. I am reminded of Uncle Nick and his homemade winemaking process. The love Victor shares with his wine is matched only by that of Uncle Nick.

I tell Victor that my Uncle Nick used to make the best wine in the family. "Many others tried and truly failed."

He smiles and says, "You must make vino with your heart and soul. Then it will be the best." Victor takes an empty bottle and fills it from the cask. We walk upstairs and enter his kitchen. It is the standard countryside kitchen with a pint-sized refrigerator, sink, stove, table, and *one* kitchen cabinet. Most kitchens are the size of an American walk-in closet and function much more efficiently than their American counterparts. Italians buy food fresh, shopping for what they will eat that day. It's simple, it's fresh, and it saves on energy consumption. Fresh food does not need to be refrigerated. Cured meats and cheese are not refrigerated. Eggs and milk not refrigerated. This is why refrigerators are the size of a shoebox from Gucci.

Now, with two juice glasses, a bottle of Victor's great homemade wine, the *Times* article, and the local phone book, our quest begins. We have Carlo's full name from the article. Judging from the picture's caption, Carlo lives near Lago Trasimeno. We further perusing the article, looking up names and calling and calling. Each time we make a call, we are given more advice on where Carlo might be. After an hour, we have made only three phone calls, because for each phone call we talk and talk and talk.

Finally, we find Carlo; he is just a ten-minute drive away. I set up an appointment to visit him the following day, along with a friend who is bilingual to help in translating. My quest for the keeper of seeds is now a reality. Praise the Lord, I will become a true Italian farmer with the help of Nick, Rose, Stefano, Victor, and now Carlo. I promise Victor that I will provide him with seeds as thanks for his assistance on my quest.

Victor and I continue to drink his wine. He explains he has rooms to rent if I need extra space when friends come to visit. We pick up our wine glasses and head off to see them. Victor's house is in town and is extremely large. Each room is more like an apartment. There are three in all—one unit with three bedrooms and the others with two bedrooms. Each unit has a kitchen and living room. The floors are well-polished terrazzo tiles and the walls a simple beige hue, hung with pictures of Venice, Roma, and Jesus. We talk about the town and how long Victor has lived here. His father built the house many years ago. Victor lived here with his family until he left for college and then went to work in Perugia. When his father died, Victor took on the chores of the farm and house. He is now retired. He used to come on the weekends, but now he stays longer, especially during the spring and fall, to prepare the vineyard and olive trees.

We spoke of the war and its effects on Villastrada. The town was on the Trasimeno Line, an offensive. A history book shows many pictures of the area, which was ravaged by the fighting between the retreating Germans and the pursuing Allies. One picture in particular depicts the English army camped out along the main street, via Patigiani. Part of Victor's house was hit during this German retreat and English offensive. The picture is a testament to the war; a large hole in the side wall of his home illustrates the depth of the war's destruction. Victor is aware that my house also was struck during the attacks. Today, the only signs of this destruction are the rubble pattern that designates the building repair. This random rubble pattern and small remnants of bullet holes are found through the countryside.

I explain that my father's family had relatives in Italy during the war and that my Uncle Augie was stationed in the European arena. I often think of the difficulty he faced, knowing at times he would be called to attack his family's homeland and possibly his family's hometown. The small town of Popoli also was attacked extensively during the war, and most of my father's paternal family was killed during an Allied air attack in March 1944. Today, Italy no longer wishes to shed the blood of its children. Italy has few children, the Italian population rate is zero; each life is a sacred gift. War has left its mark on this country, and Italians have chosen not to forget, lest they relive the past.

We move to a lighter conversation—more history of the town and Victor's family. We realize it is getting late and Rose soon will be calling "Giovanna," so Victor and I walk down to the wine cellar. He pours two bottles of wine for me to take home. We bid each other *bona sera*, kiss, and promise to meet tomorrow at the market. I am now giddy with the prospect of having found the "heirloom seed farmer." All is right with the world. I feel like breaking into song, as so many Italians do for no apparent reason, other than that the joy inside them must surface.

Light with wine, life, and jet lag, I walk down the driveway to the farm. The clouds fill the sky over the fields in early evening. The view is a majestic display of nature, the fields budding with the new crop and the smoke reminding me of last year's pruning of the olive branches. The world is right; the bells toll. It is later than I thought.

To me, Uncle Nick and Aunt Lena were my "grandparents," as my parental grandparents passed away prior to my arrival on this planet. Uncle Nick and Aunt Lena filled that void. When my mother was ill, they came and took care of us. Their children were older and married. Kindness was their strength, and love was their voice. I think about them. They remind me of Rose and Stefano, the only exception being that they did not have enough land to work, as Rose and Stefano do today. Aunt Lena tended to the house and cooking. Uncle Nick tended to what land he had and worked as a mason. The two became one. Their house was everyone's house. Uncle Nick started a masonry company that is still going strong today, run first by his sons and now his grandsons.

As I look around town and see the beautiful church made of brick and the terra cotta roof tiles, the voice of my ancestry follows me. Who made these bricks and tiles? When I look at the rows of brick, I realize each brick has a story to tell—a day's work by a man with a family and a life. What events of daily life affected them? We should be eternally grateful for the craftsmanship and dedication. The men's talents and labors adorn this country and many cities in the United States. Italy humbles us, reminding us of those who walked before us and those who lived life and preserved what existed. Italy teaches us to repair, not destroy.

I think for a moment, and I return to the beauty and joy of this land. A smile appears on my face. Mark Twain, in his *The Innocents Abroad*, was harsh on Italy. The women, in fact, do not have beards, and they do use soap, contrary to Twain's observations, though the Italians don't shower with the obsessive-compulsive nature of Americans, who do no physical work yet need two showers a day. Maybe Americans are attempting to wash away their lack of connection between those individuals who feed them, the American farmer. I feel decadent because there are three showers in my farmhouse. My justification might be that the showers are merely faucets projecting out of the bathroom wall and onto a floor. A single drain is all that gathers the water.

The sound of an opera comes from my neighbor's house. The dog that lives up on the second floor uses the roof as her backyard. She is the guardian of the driveway, constantly barking at anyone who passes by. I call out for her to stop, saying, *"Basta, Lula!"* She continues on as if she doesn't understand a word. I fear one day she will fall off the roof in a moment of frenzied excitement.

Little green lizards run for shelter as the sun dips closer to the horizon. Here the sun lingers longer than in most places. It is as if there is no urgency to end the day, and I thank her for that.

While the walk is short, my thoughts are long. There is work to be done and friends to greet. *Grazie, Italia.*

I have lingered long with Victor. The church bells are the town's clock, marking the passing of every half hour. Rose and Stefano are coming down the driveway. The spring pruning is delicate work; I am not yet ready to be taught this art. The fruit trees are planted and the day's work done without stress, anger, or bitterness. We kiss and wait to greet tomorrow.

I reach the house and walk through the opened door. A small bird is sitting on the dining room table; crumbs from the bread I left on the table will supply her with food for the evening. I always leave the doors and windows open during the warm months. The house sits in such a position that a fresh breeze always gently fills the rooms. The starlings fill the trees, and their voices are an overwhelming sound, Pavarotti and starlings—beautiful. The rooster that lives in the multispecies pavilion and can't carry a note attempts to call an end to the day. He is always off, both in pitch and timing. I'm sure the rabbits and goats wish he would lose what is left of his vocal cords. Or maybe they are deaf to the sound. The sun has finished its day's work, and the moon waits patiently for its lead role. The opera still plays.

Chapter 5
Translating

Every Italian house renovation has a first-contractor story. I believe it is a rite of passage while restoring any property. Without Pietro and Sarah, my friends from Arezzo, my home would stand as it stood three years ago—basically, a demolition mass of rubble without doors, windows, fireplace, sink, and electricity. So when Pietro and Sarah offered their expertise and help, I jumped for joy.

"Yes, please, yes!" was my response.

Both were diligent in keeping me from complete despair. They knew the business of restoration. When they lived in southern Italy, they purchased and restored old homes. They were seasoned at Italian restoration. My house had been gutted and the pigsties half demolished when the renovation was ordered stopped. As I said, the first contractor had a different interpretation of the English language. Pietro diligently labored to find new workers and contractors. This task was no easy feat, as the house was in ruins. Few contractors were willing to take on the responsibility of repairing what had been destroyed by the first one, but Pietro found a local contractor who was perfect for the job. We all agreed that Pietro would stop on his way to and from Roma, where he was currently working, to check on the progress of the project and answer any concerns. It was Pietro and Sarah would ensure the renovation would be properly executed and provide me a beautifully restored Italian farmhouse. I love my home—with beautiful lights from their Murano glass shop in Arezzo. Despite the endless hours of traveling to the antique flea market on the first of each month in Arezzo, we attempted to find just the right pieces of furniture there to fill this space. They made my nightmare a dream. I will be grateful forever.

I was introduced to Sarah and Pietro through Sarah's brother Bill, who lived on the Island back in New York. Bill informed me that his sister had gone to Italy twenty-five years ago, fallen in love, and never returned.

My first venture to the flea market was almost three years ago. The first contractor had promised the house would be done in a few months. This is where I believe the translation between his English and my Italian first diverged. Believing the house would be completed on time, I traveled to Arezzo to meet Sarah and Pietro. We had lunch and then went off to the flea market—this was my first family lunch in the "city." I arrived at their apartment and walked the four flights up. Outside their apartment door, beautiful potted plants lined the landing, and I wondered how they managed to transport the large terra cotta pots up all those flights of stairs. I thought they must be superhuman. I knocked on the door.

Sarah greeted me and led me into the apartment. The apartment was beautiful and the views stunning; the terrace was filled with life and the air filled with aromas of lunch. Pietro came from the kitchen to greet me. I handed them some wine and cheese that I had brought for the meal. The kitchen table was adorned with antipasti, water, and wine. This not only was a gastronomic delight but also a visual sight for the eyes. (Pietro and Sarah both are great chefs in their own right. Sarah claims Pietro keeps his cooking a secret, never revealing his ingredients or herbs, but Sarah never allows anyone to watch her while in the process of preparing a meal.) Pietro poured a glass of wine for us, and we walked out to the terrace. The sunlight filled every corner, and large terra cotta pots filled with vegetables and herbs lined the walls and balcony. The sight was visually stunning and aromatically intoxicating. I felt as if I was outside the farm in Umbria, not on a fourth-story terrace in the city.

I returned to the kitchen and sat down. Sarah and Pietro had just finished preparing the first and second plate. "So you know Bill from the Island?" Sarah asked.

"Yes, when I mentioned I'd bought a house in Italy, he told me about your living in Arezzo and suggested I contact you for possible help with the house."

Sarah smiled and responded, "I lived in Southampton for a while and was actually born out there. Pietro and I go back to the United States to see my mom; she lives on Cape Cod."

"Where were you born?" I asked.

"Eastern Long Island in October 1955," she responded.

It took about two seconds to realize we were born ten days apart. We broke into laughter, and from that day on we have called each other *me sorella*—my sister. At that moment, like so many moments in Italy, I was at home with my family.

"Do you have children?" Sarah asked.

"I have a small pod of children, five to be exact—four daughters and one son. I feel sorry for him. He is always surrounded by a pack of females."

"You have five children?" Sarah questioned in disbelief.

"The magic number is five. They range in age from twenty-one to eleven. I had a ten-year run in the baby-making business." I jokingly replied. "Pietro, where is your family from?"

"I come from southern Italy, but I cannot be your brother," he laughed. "I was born here. But you can be … how do you say it? My sister-by-law." We all broke into laughter. "*Mangia*," Pietro ordered, in his soft Italian accent.

We enjoyed the bounty of antipasti that landscaped the table. The view from the kitchen window was of the *centro* of the walled city; specifically, the doma of the cathedral. The town's church bell towers and the rustic terra cotta roofs finish the palate. The window frame creates an imaginary frame for what one might believe to be a Renaissance painting. The church bells began to toll. They informed me that their son and daughter, Aldo and Alessandra, soon would be returning from school. Schoolchildren eat lunch at home, not in a school cafeteria. It was Saturday, but the Italian school week starts on Monday and continues through today.

Dismayed, I said, "Americans can't get their children to go to school five days a week. How do the Italians keep their children in school for six?"

Pietro smiled. "Education is important in Italy. If a student doesn't do well in lower and secondary school—a five year program—he doesn't go on to college. It's really that simple. Education is a privilege."

I looked at Pietro and Sarah and gave the only possible reply. "Americans have lost that concept. The students think it's the school's privilege if they show up. It's crazy." They nodded in agreement.

A look of surrender overcame us. The dining room table was set. We left the comforts of the kitchen and moved to the elegant dining room. The dining room overlooked the terrace and its beautiful gardens, with large windows that allowed the fragrances and breeze inside. The sunlight filtered in through the lace curtains and created shadows that danced along the plaster walls. Pietro was listening to his favorite music—opera. He joined in at various moments, singing with his rich baritone voice.

Pietro and Sarah sat at either end of the table. I sat at Pietro's left. We talked about the progress of the restoration of Olivetta. I admitted I was concerned with some items that were missing—original doors, windows, gates, shutters, andirons and whatever else seemed to have walked away from the restoration site. I looked at Pietro and asked, "Is it customary for neighbors to believe that a reconstruction site is just an open used-materials site?"

Pietro and Sarah looked at each other with that knowing look, much like a parent has when a child has asked a question for which the answer is best left a mystery.

I laughed and said, "I now understand. I had a demolished house with the added disadvantage of providing all my neighbors with any and all materials they might need for restoring or repairing their houses without any cost to them."

"Ah, that is normal." Pietro said.

Aldo and Alessandra arrived home. They were dressed as if going to Sunday school. I felt as if I was at a high-end retail store in New York. Before me was the perfectly dressed family in a perfectly decorated Italian home. I waited for Ozzie and Harriet to walk in at any moment to join us.

I was introduced to Alessandra and Aldo. They both spoke fluent English and Italian. When they spoke English, they had Sarah's Boston accent; when they spoke Italian, they had the proper Roman accent and grammar. A pain came over me. I could have spoken Italian as they did if my mother had just allowed my father and his family to speak the language. Did it really matter that Grandma called my mother *pazzo, pazzo*?

Alessandra and Aldo joined us at the dining room table and provided an account of the morning activities—schoolwork and friends—and then the plans for the afternoon. Lunch began; Aldo and Alessandra soon cleared the antipasti and brought the first plate to the table. We laughed and talked about school in Italy. Aldo was a great rugby player and provided me with the highlights of the past season. I promised that the next time I was in Arezzo and he was playing, I would be delighted to watch. Sarah, Pietro, and I continued our conversation on the restoration of Olivetta and discussed what we needed to purchase at the market.

Alessandra and Aldo cleared the *primo platto* from the table and returned with the *secondo platto*. I was stuffed and could not possibly consume another morsel, I gently declined the offering. We continue our conversation on school, sports, and life. The *secondo platto* was finished. Alessandra and Aldo cleared the table. The next course arrived—fruit and cheese plates. Pietro picked up a *mele* (apple) and began to peel the skin. Then he cut it in half and then quarters. He removed the seeds and offered a piece to everyone. For a moment, I was at a loss for words. The last person to do this for me was my father. He was in charge of peeling and distributing apples.

I looked at Pietro and said, "My father always did that."

Pietro looked at me and asked, "Did what?"

"Peeled apples for us at dinner."

"All Italian fathers do this," Pietro said.

"It's been a long time since my father was here," I said. "Thank you for this gift of remembrance."

We continued with fruit and cheese. The meal was not over. Next, Pietro's favorite course, *vin santo*—the gentle, sweet Italian dessert wine with biscotti. Intoxicated with food and now the sweet taste of *vin santo*, we finished with the food portion of the meal. Alessandra and Aldo again cleared the table. They returned with espresso. Pietro, Sarah, and I talked about the flea market again and our goal and direction. We agreed that the list of needs was long, and it was easier to list what I did *not* need.

Before we headed off, it was time for siesta, and I truly understood the meaning of the "need for siesta." Our minds were asleep; it was now time for our bodies to follow suit. Sarah prepared a bed for me on the large sofa in the living room. I curled up. The opera was still playing, and it lulled me to sleep. It seemed only a few short minutes later when I heard Sarah say, "It's time to go to the market."

We dressed for the cool weather and began our descent down the four flights of stairs. When we opened the door, a rush of wind brushed our faces and erased any hint of slumber that might have remained in our beings.

The Arezzo flea market engulfed the walled city. Vendors lined the streets and alleys. Every square inch was filled with an object for sale, from a single piece of antique crystal to a twenty-foot hand-carved front door façade. This month's market was under a veil of yesterday's unusual snow. There was no snow removal equipment and no road salt in this region of Italy—the last snow had appeared over a hundred years ago. Italians, being a culture of inventors, provided a simple solution. The vendors and shopkeepers decided to use coffee beans for traction for vehicles and individuals. Yes, the streets were covered with coffee beans. The smell was fantastic, and for a moment I felt as if I was in a café. The contrast of the white snow with the rich, dark coffee beans was a visual delight. The success of this snow removal venture, however, was minimal. We walked through the crowded market past vendor after vendor. Sarah, whom I call the "pit bull" of flea markets, had an instinct for bargains. We came to a beautiful hand-carved chestnut bed that was two hundred years old. I looked at Sarah and Pietro.

"Is 180 euros the correct price?" I asked. This bed certainly was worth 1,000 euros. "Let's buy it."

Sarah said, "Just one moment." Within three sentences, she had the price reduced to 150 euros, and the vendor agreed to deliver it the next day to their Murano glass shop. I could not control my delight. Sarah gave me that Cheshire Cat smile—the bargaining had been successful.

The afternoon moved on, and it was time for Sarah to open their shop. Pietro stayed with me to continue our sojourn. We found a beautiful antique farm table, but it was expensive—500 euros. Pietro knew the vendor and began negotiations.

When negations were done, Pietro turned to me and said, "Tomorrow we will offer him half the price. It will be the last day of the market, and he will not want to take it back to his shop."

I still believed the price was a fraction of what it would cost in the United States. I asked, "Are you sure?"

Pietro smiled and assured me, "It will be fine."

The day was ending, and it was time for the vendors to close.

"Closing" for flea market vendors meant throwing a tarp over their goods and tying some string or rope around the tables.

I looked at Pietro and said, "Are they leaving everything out on the street tonight?"

His response was simple. "*Si.*"

I was in disbelief. "What if someone steals it?"

Pietro now smiled again and said, "Who would dare try to steal this?"

I responded, "People, of course."

He laughed. "These people will not steal from each other. They protect each other."

We walked down to the piazza, where the cafés were full of people. The café owners had placed heaters to allow customers to remain outside, even if the weather was not agreeable.

I looked at Pietro and asked, "An espresso or glass of wine?"

"*Si.*"

We sat down at a small café. The town was filled with voices. In the late afternoon, warm amber lights filled the piazza. We ordered *vino rosso* and reviewed our purchases and strategy for tomorrow. Our order arrived. To my amazement, it was not merely *vino rosso* but a small sampler of antipasto. I looked at Pietro and inquired if he had requested this. He looked at me and laughed. "We are in the city now, not in your little village. In the city at the end of the day, the cafés provide samples of antipasto to accompany *vino.*"

I looked at him and said, "Civilized."

We finished and paid the *conto*. I thanked Pietro for such a wonderful afternoon, and we bid each other *buona sera*. We agreed to meet at the café in the morning and return to the street vendor to make our final offer on the farm table. *Baci, baci.*

As I walked back to my hotel, I looked down the now-empty streets. The crowds restricted themselves to the café and to the shops just below where the flea market stopped. There were no armed security guards, just a rudimentary small fence and a visual signal that the street was closed for the evening.

Too excited to remain in my room, I ventured out and found a café for a cup of espresso—it was too early for dinner. I carried with me my restoration notebook, and now I reviewed the basic needs for my farmhouse. I was anxious about the table, but then a voice came to me—*piano, piano,* slow. I would have to wait until tomorrow to purchase my dream table. I would be patient. I heard the church bells in the distance, added a few notes to my list of "to-dos" and crossed off what was done.

The hotel had recommended a restaurant near the train station. It was tiny, with a large fire pit at the back of the dining room. The hostess showed me to a table off to the side and pulled the chair out for me to sit. There were no families here, but there were a number of older couples. Many of the individuals looked as if they were there for the flea market, and this was the place to end a day of hard negotiations. I ordered my wine and water, and the waitress handed me a menu. I took a closer look at the room. The fire in front of me was actually a stove. In front of the stove was a large section of meat—boar, rabbit, deer, pig? The waitress returned and informed me of the night's special—wild boar. It is excellent.

Grazie, e possible pasta e insalta? (Thank you, no. Is it possible to have pasta and a salad?) The waitress responded.

"Of course that would not be a problem, but wouldn't I have a second plate?" she inquired.

"*Grazie, non.*"

I was in a restaurant that was a carnivore's delight. I waited for my pasta to arrive and watched the butcher carefully slice sections of meat—each dish was cut to order and prepared directly in front of the customer. I was amazed at the skill and precision of the butcher. It is one thing to have dinner prepared tableside, but here, customers actually watched the butchering and cooking process.

A gentleman sitting at the table next to me asked, "Have you been to the market?"

I responded, "*Si*. Are you here for the market to buy or to sell?"

He informed me that he and his companion were equestrians and had been at the equestrian show that afternoon at the world-renowned center just outside of town. We continued speaking and realized that we all shared English as our primary language. They had traveled from England and Scotland for the equestrian competition. I mentioned that my children were avid riders.

They invited me to watch the show the next day. I thanked them for the invitation but explained I was unable to attend. "Next time you are in Arezzo," I said, "I would certainly attend and, if possible, bring my two daughters."

My pasta arrived. The gentlemen had finished their second plate and were waiting for *dolce*. One of the gentlemen took his laptop out of his bag and asked if I would like to view the video of today's events.

"Certainly, I would enjoy that very much."

As the first rider started the course, the gentlemen began their critique. I became aware that people at two additional tables had participated in the event. It was a gathering of the men of the Arezzo Classic. As if on cue, everyone took out a laptop. We pushed the tables together, and each laptop displayed the video of one rider. It was fantastic to watch these men competing on a world-class level. Each offered advice and constructive criticism to the other. Occasionally, they would ask me, "What do you think."

My only response was, "You are all too professional for my amateur eye."

It was time to end our meal. I exchanged e-mail addresses with my new friends and promised to keep in touch. As I left the café, the streets were quiet and empty. I entered the hotel, greeted the concierge, and took the steps up to my room.

I was sleeping soundly when I heard the phone ring, and it startled me at first. *Where am I? Why is there a phone ringing?* I pulled my senses together and looked around the room. *Arezzo, the flea market*. It was time to meet Pietro at the café.

At the café the tables were full of eager antique hunters. I sat down, ordered my cappuccino, and waited. The sun on this day had replaced the monochromatic gray of yesterday morning. I still smelled the crushed coffee beans that served yesterday as traction for the slippery roads. Pietro arrived and ordered a cappuccino. We talked about where we would explore first. He decided to go to the vendor with the table just before lunch. "If we go earlier, he will not give us a good price because he will think we are anxious." When I assured Pietro that I was anxious, he said, "No, Giovanna, that is not so."

We found large, beautiful pieces that were part of an old alchemist's cupboard, housing mysteries to cure all aliments. Pietro and I looked at each other—we loved the piece. One of the pieces had been completely restored; the other still was in its original condition. The hand-painted labels, almost invisible, displayed only a portion of the original lettering. The piece was rough and perfect for my country farmhouse. Pietro began his negotiations, which meant waving of hands up and down. His voice and the vendor's rose and fell; the church bell deafened their cadence. The vendor agreed on a price and said that he would keep the piece for two months. Pietro agreed to a fifty euro deposit. We left the large piazza and moved back up the narrow streets. The streets were alive, taking on their own life, not only with vendors and prospective clients, but also with dogs and street performers. It was a carnival. At the farm-table vendor's stall, yesterday's discussion continued. I understood only a portion of the verbal negotiation, but I did understand the visual and audio—hands moving rapidly, voices at first *piano* and then building to *crescendo*. When the volume increased this meant someone didn't understand or more did not agree. I could tell from the visual cues that there was a victory for Pietro and only a partial victory for the vendor. *Bravo*. When all was said and done, Pietro got a much better price, and the vendor agreed to keep the piece until my house was ready. I looked at Pietro and asked what the *crescendo* had indicated.

"He wanted you to leave a deposit," Pietro laughed.

"Why didn't you want to leave a deposit with him?" I asked.

"Because ... how do you say? I did not think it was right for him to ask. We should only shake his hand."

A smile came over my face. It was time to celebrate. We went to the café had a glass of *vino*. Pietro had to return to their apartment to prepare the lunch. He insisted that I stay for lunch, but I had to decline. ...

I realize I have been dreaming.

Chapter 6
Learning

The starlings have begun their end-of-the-day song, and my memory gradually dims. Twilight at the farm is the most precious moment of the day. It is as if it's choreographed by Isadora Duncan and painted by Michelangelo. The clouds move in from the west as the sun gracefully plays against the land and sky. Shadows are cast through the branches of the olive trees and across the vast green fields before me. While all of this magic plays out on the land, the sun adds to the beauty by creating heaven in the sky. Looking up, I imagine the existence of the spirit of the universe. Sunbeams jet from behind cumulous clouds and juxtapose against dark gray thunderheads. The events last for two hours, never repeating or boring me. I often have wondered, when studying the great masters, how their perception of the celestial realm was possible. It took Olivetta to open my eyes and my spiritual being to the beauty and majesty of the world and of heaven. For me, this is the time of the day when the past, present, and future blend. It truly is a meditative state of awareness and unity.

I pour myself a glass of Victor's wine and take a bottle of Pellegrino upstairs to sit outside on the *terrazzo* (terrace). This small space is my end-of-the-day haven. I know I will walk up to the café in two hours, but this is the time when the heavens and earth become one, when the sky kisses the earth—*tra il Lusco e il Brusco*—and the day's work has come to an end. Working in Italy is not like working. To me, using the word *work* in Italy is an, oxymoron you really don't work, you live. You garden, paint, varnish, clean, and care for what others have cared for and given you, whether purchased or from the family. I sit here in my world of heaven and earth.

I see Gina walking down the driveway, and I go to greet her. Rose has Aunt Lena's personality, but Gina has Lena's physique. When Gina is outside, she wears her scarf wrapped carefully over her head, tied with a small knot. She always wears a buttoned-up sweater, skirt, black stockings, the only style of shoe Italian country women seem to wear, and, depending on the time of the day, an apron. What they all share is a sign of contentment in accomplishment. Their two hands always are placed ceremoniously on their cheeks, followed by a surprised look and then a smile. Yes, this is contentment. My childhood is now in front of me. I am home.

Gina claims she has come to thank me and to see the house. I say, "This will always be your house. I hope I have done it justice." She smiles, both hands on her checks, and says, "*Belle, brava.*" My heart is full of joy, and I break into a smile.

We have a glass of wine and some fruit and cheese. We laugh, and she tells stories of how the pigs use to live where we are sitting. The pigs' feeding trough were reclaimed, they are now incorporated into the fireplace mantels and the kitchen counter. The old green Italian doors and shutters are still here. The old shutters are the doors for the cabinets under the kitchen counter. The ladder that once provided access to the attic is a focal point of the kitchen, serving well as a repository for dishes. She talks about living here with her family. They had a sink with running water, a technological breakthrough of its time. The old fireplace provided all necessary heat and was used for cooking. Inside the large fireplace was a small bench off to the left that allowed one to climb in and warm up or dry clothing and shoes. Being with

Gina is a pleasure; she is so gentle. I beg her to stay longer and share her life and stories. She explains it is time for her to return home and start preparing dinner. I offer her a ride up the steep hill, but she gently declines.

I realize this country swaddles me. It provides me with heart, soul, and family. This is my childhood, and I relive it with relish. This is my voice and my reason. The past has walked in front of me, yet the past now carries me to my future. I sway not from the seeds of my grandparents or from the soil and soul that built my life. I sit overlooking this farm I call home, and I am welcomed. There are no bitter arguments. Friends and family have walked on these sacred grounds, and now they welcome my return.

It is hard not to feel the past in the present. On the last All Souls' Eve, which is called Halloween in America, Elaine, a friend from Ireland, visited with her dog, Lassie. The cemetery was alive with candles, flowers, and people. All Souls' Eve in Italy is a day of respect; it is not a day of candy and pranks. Elaine and I talked of the traditions of this holiday and of the respect for those who walked before us and how they gently cared for our needs. We decided to visit the cemetery and pay our respects to the past keepers of Villastrada. With wine glasses in hand, we walked the steep, dark road. Before we arrived, we could smell the sweet scent of flowers and candles. A warm glow seemed to emanate from the hallowed ground. When we arrived, the gates were open, and the image before us was truly heavenly. The walls were filled with candles and flowers. There must have been five hundred small glowing lights. As we entered, something beyond description swept through our souls. We walked through the corridors, stopping to read each inscription. On each headstone was a picture and a brief story of the life that had been lived, a highlight of memories never to be forgotten or lost. We looked closely at the black-and-white photographs of faces that shined back at us, illuminated by the flickering of the candlelight.

As we walked on, I looked at Elaine and asked, "Where is your wine glass? Did you lose it?"

"No, I didn't lose it. I left it with Sophia. I asked her if it was okay."

"Who is Sophia, and when did you give it to her?" I inquired.

"Sophia is over there. Remember, she was the schoolteacher. I asked her if I could leave my glass with her while we walked through the cemetery." she calmly stated.

I smiled, and we continued on, stopping to pay our respects to each soul. The cemetery is not a cemetery in the American sense. Here, it is filled with life. Photographs of every soul, candles, flowers, and gifts adorn all the tombs; every soul is venerated, every life acknowledged. Walking with reverence, our hearts stood still. I looked at Elaine, an international journalist, and asked, "Can you write this moment?"

She replied, "This is a moment one has to live."

It was a moment lost to this world. We walked through the illuminated rows of life still honored and still alive. The church bells tolled in a sacred voice. Aromas filled the rest of this exceptional spiritual moment. We bowed and crossed ourselves, asking God to bless these souls. Then we walked back through the iron gates. Our journey back to the farm was in silence. We had neither the ability nor the desire to speak. We did not wish to break the magic of the moment. On our way back, I thought of Rinny, Lena, and Nick. I thought of how differently we mourn in America.

I do not go often to see Lena and Nick at the cemetery. I'm not often in Greenport. When I am on the Island, I do go to see Dad and Rinny. What's different, though, is the Catholic cemetery on the island, does not allow statues, and you can't light candles. If you leave anything, it must be small and not get in the way of the lawnmower. I have received letters warning me to stop bringing the angel statue to my daughter's grave. In fact, the last time I placed the statue between my dad and Rinny, it was confiscated. When I returned the following day, there was no angel. How sad. I wish Rinny and Dad were here, where their lives would always be remembered.

Now, in the darkness, the gentle tears of grief roll down my face. I then realized Rinny and Dad were here and will always be here. As long as I can breathe, I will remember them.

I think back to Halloween as a child. My American mother insisted that all American traditions be upheld. It was her small attempt to water down the Italian traditions. The first order of Halloween was the costume. My mother was obsessed with picking the right costume. Her thought was that we all had to match as a unit. After what seemed like hours, we were ready. We would pile into the family's paneled wagon, board the ferry and we were off to Greenport to see my father's family. My mother took it upon herself to indoctrinate every member of my father's Italian family into American culture or, more specifically, American holidays. First stop was always Aunt Eddie and Uncle Doc's. They owned a small Italian food market that was loaded with one-cent candy. We would run in, truly, as kids in a candy store. Our bags were full before we left, but it wasn't just the filling of the bags that was our pleasure. It was the time immersed in festivities and laughing. Uncle Doc and Aunt Eddie always pretended they were either frightened or unaware of our true identity. The game went on for minutes and was a true delight. When we had filled our bags and bellies, we ran out as fast out as we had run in. Next stop was Uncle Nick and Aunt Lena's house. Aunt Mary was always there for this event. We would run up to the door, dropping all or part of our costumes. We wanted into this haven, to see them all sitting at the kitchen table, waiting for us. We knocked as hard and as fast as we could, while they pretended not to hear, and we begged and pleaded, saying, "Trick or treat." as loudly as we could.

Then we would hear, "We don't know who 'Trick or Treat' is."

We'd be just about to burst with anticipation when Uncle

Nick opened the door. Aunts Lena and Mary pretended to be startled, frightened, and totally amused, holding back their smiles holding the sides of their faces with their hands, and then saying *"Mama Mia"* Once in the house, it was time to shed thecostumes and enjoy *dolce*. We laughed, ate, and laughed some more. The world was right. Then, Aunt Lena would say, "It's time to go to church."

We always were confused by this. Why would they be going to church on Halloween? Afraid to ask for fear of having to attend mass, we kissed, hugged, and then departed. It is only now I understand the true meaning for them and for this great culture. Now I attend mass and light the candle of respect, remembrance, hope, and knowledge that they imparted to me.

I pour some wine and look out at the landscape. There is a melancholy, a sadness with these thoughts. A smile comes to my face. If there is death, there must have been a birth, and I think about the birthday parties of my youth. As our birthdays neared, the anticipation almost became unbearable. The celebration had more to do with the Italian need to celebrate life. The joy of a new being coming into the world was paramount, and it still is today in Italy. Birth means everything to an Italian family. There is the ritual blessing of the baby, the kissing, and the sign of the cross.

When growing up, celebrating my birthday started with a new outfit. Choosing the outfit was always a process; it took the better part of an afternoon and meant a trip to the mainland. My mother was an avid shopper, and this was no exception. Each "outfit" option had to be critically examined. The dressing room was filled with what Mom thought was right, and what the birthday girl thought was right. When the final decision was made, which basically meant my mother was happy, we would move on to the shoe store. The shoe choice was patent leather, as far as my mother was concerned. If the birthday girl was lucky enough and old enough, a high heel was added to the mix. Not to be forgotten and certainly never overlooked were the ankle socks with a lace accent.

The birthday party would start promptly at 6 p.m. The cake always was hidden until the moment the candles were lit and lights were dimmed. The appointed hour provided everyone with a chance to freshen up from their day's work and prepare for the celebration. The anticipation of opening the presents was painful. It always seemed to take too long to eat dinner, too long to clean up, and worst of all, too long for the grownups to stop talking and get the cake on the table. Gifts from my father's family were always handmade—a scarf, mittens, or a new shawl. The love that went into these gifts was reflected in the loving faces of the maker and the receiver. I think of the year Aunt Lena made me a quilt. It was a rite of passage. The joy was seeing which colors and pattern she had picked out to capture my personality (or at least Aunt Lena's perception of my character). Lena spent hours making this quilt. It was a true sign of her love. My quilt was a variegated green; it was warm and beautiful. I have now retired it to the cedar chest, as it has become tattered and frayed from many years of use. I can't bear to throw it out.

It has been a long time since those sacred parties. My memory, I am sure, embraces only the pleasant moments. I can remember the cakes. Yes, the cakes. There were always two—one was the desired chocolate for the children; the other was a more traditional almond Italian cake for the adults. Mom would hire the local professional photographer to capture every moment. The cousins, aunts, and uncles surrounded the large kitchen table. The long Formica and stainless steel table was decorated with a tablecloth. We didn't have a formal dining room at that time. All events, holidays, and festivities were held in the kitchen. Party favors and balloons filled the space. An hour of rubbing balloons on our heads to get them to "stick" to the ceiling or walls was a prerequisite to this festivity. There always was a sign that read in large capital letters, *BUON COMPLEANNO* (happy birthday). It was always a happy birthday. Everyone was dressed up. The cake stood on a musical cake plate that went in a circle and played "Happy Birthday." The fun was listening to the Italians sing "Happy Birthday" in Italian, while the Americans sang in English. Somehow or other, it all seemed to work. It also was the only time Italian was spoken in my "mother's" house. Later on, the birthdays faded as age took its toll on my father's family. The once-festive celebrations turned into more of a statement of mortality. There was a realization of who no longer was there. In my life, there was the first realization of Uncle V, Aunt Mary, Uncle Nick, and then Aunt Lena. It was at this point that the celebrations almost stopped. I believe it was too painful for everyone. To lose so many family members in such a few short years was harder than any of us wanted to admit or could bear.

What changed all of this was the birth of the first grandchild. I had the first grandchild, and that was a celebration of profound proportion. It lasted a week. Main Street had a sign reading "It's a girl." The christening was more like a wedding than a small religious celebration. Fourteen months later, I produced the first male in my father's family since my brother's birth. Again, this was cause for celebration of life and the renewal of a family. Knowing that my older children would enjoy the same love and care I received when young, I was filled with joy and the hope of never losing these ties. Knowing that my children would be able to understand and grow up in a loving and caring Italian family comforted me.

The only other birthday party that matched my own was my father's. Dad loved birthdays, and his was always around the time of the World Series. When the Yankees or Red Socks were in the series, there was no holding back. Everyone had a mitt, glove, baseball, or bat. The rivalry between the two teams has long stood in our family. The aunts and uncles who lived in Massachusetts were all Red Sox fans. My cousin was a sports writer who used to cover the Red Sox games. Everyone in New

York was a Yankee fan. It is a rivalry that continues to this day. There was always the story of the Babe curse. Every year, before the birthday cake candles were blown out, the Babe story was told. I'm not sure if my father did this because he wanted us to always remember or if he had just forgotten he had told the story the year before. Our singing "Happy Birthday" was soon replaced by "Take Me Out to the Ball Game." My father's family became truly American every time baseball season started.

My first real Italian birthday party was in Italy—my fiftieth birthday—and I wanted to celebrate it in my farmhouse. The first contractor had promised all would be done on time. I certainly should have known better. The invitations were sent. The celebration would last three days. In a true Italian tradition, if it's your birthday and you want a party, you pay.

As the celebration time approached, it became painfully apparent that the party would not and could not take place at Olivetta. Olivetta still stood with no doors, windows, electricity, heat, or plumbing. This was more than a small-fix problem. I urgently contacted a friend of a friend who operated a house rental program in Italy. My problem was that I needed a house for twenty people and needed it in two weeks. Challenges are my forte. After numerous calls and e-mails and a lot of Lady Luck, a location was secured. Instead of Villastrada, the celebration would take place in Cetona. I sent new directions to all the guests. The party was on.

I arrived a few days prior to guests and family in the event of a problem. Pietro and I met with the agent in the grand piazza in Cetona. Pietro had lived in Cetona many years ago, but the town hadn't changed in nine hundred years, so we expected everything still would be as it was then. We arrived early and decided to have a glass of wine. Pietro informed me there was a "local workers' bar" just around the corner—the workers' bar (actually, a café) charged barely fifty cents for a glass of wine.

Pietro ordered two *vinos* and we sat down outside at the small tables that lined the building. Above our heads, proudly displayed, was the sign of the workers' party. I was the only woman at the bar, something that happened often. The tables were filled with men all dressed in their country attire. The talk was political and animated. I realized that all conversation in Italy is animated. I asked Pietro, "What are they so upset about?"

He smiled. "They are not upset; they are angry with Berlusconi. He uses all the people's money for himself." Pietro pointed to a large sign with block letters that stated the recent transgressions of Prime Minister Silvio Berlusconi. I laughed. We drank our wine and enjoyed the theatrical performance around us. The church bell rang—it was time to meet the rental agent. We bid *ciao* to the gentlemen sitting against the wall outside the bar and headed to the piazza.

Angela, the agent, was on time. She was a small woman with limited English-speaking ability. I wasn't worried, as Pietro could translate for me. Angela said she would take us to the property and show us the mechanics of the house. We followed her in our car. The drive was not exactly short. In fact, at one point I said to Pietro, "Will anyone find this?"

We turned off the paved road and continued down a long, winding dirt road. Actually, it appeared we were driving into the middle of a plowed field. After another five minutes, I was about to surrender any plans for a birthday celebration. I envisioned having friends lost in the Umbrian countryside, knocking on doors, asking for help to pull their cars out of the freshly plowed fields.

We finally arrived. The house was perched high on a hilltop field with an olive grove surrounding it. There was a mechanical gate at the entrance to the driveway. *What possible purpose would this gate serve?* I wondered. *Ward off herds of wild boar or impress Americans?*

We walked through the house; in fact, it was two complete houses plus a pool house—enough room for everyone. Twenty-four people easily could sleep here. The only problem that lurked in our minds was how anyone would find this place. With the proverbial gratuities exchanged, Pietro and I were left to establish a plan.

Italians love their plans, but no one sticks to the plan—they just acknowledge a plan exists. Our plan was that there was no possible plan for getting my guests out here in the country, short of posting a sign at the end of the long, winding dirt driveway that read "Giovanna's Celebration. Follow the breadcrumbs on the side of the road."

Pietro needed to return home. I took him to the Chiusi station to catch the train.

I decided I needed to find something that directed my guests down this long road. A thought came to mind—balloons. The plan was to give guests an American reference point, something that stuck out in the Italian countryside. The market had just what I needed—well, almost what I needed. It didn't have the poster board to make a sign. I decided to tape letter-size papers together to make one large sign. Driving back to Cetona, I was proud of my simple yet functional solution. I would design the sign and attach the balloons at the beginning of the driveway early tomorrow afternoon, when most of the guests would be arriving. I still faced, however, the problem of how to direct them to this house—Angela's directions were too confusing.

The next day, I stopped at the market and picked up the necessities for lunch before going to the Chiusi train station, where my daughter, her fiancé, and my son were to arrive. I wasn't sure how we would all fit in my Fiat Panda, which was the size of a Prada boot box, but we would make it work.

I must have forgotten how Americans travel. Their luggage was piled a mile high along the entrance of the station. I parked and began the magic of fitting too much into too little space. They all had a suitcase beneath them and on top of them. With a prayer to God, Santa Rose, Saint Francis, and Buddha, everyone fit into the car. Once at the house—and looking much like a Volkswagen commercial from the early sixties—we piled out (rather, we opened the doors and fell out). We marched into the house as if a caravan of crusaders.

I prepared lunch while everyone checked out their rooms and unpacked their luggage. My lunch was simpler than most Italian lunches. I limited it to pasta, meat, salad, and *dolce.* After lunch, it was siesta time. The weary travelers returned to their chambers for a long-awaited sleep. I cleaned up while they rested.

After napping Louis, my soon-to-be son-in-law, decided to light a fire in the fireplace, with great intentions. He took paper, cardboard, and anything else that might burn and placed it in the enormous hearth. The result was a basic failure, but Louis would not surrender. After a long struggle—and a great deal of smoke—the fire roared.

I was concerned that it was getting late, and four of my guests had not arrived. It was hard enough to find the house in the daytime, and now it was pitch-black out. At one of the French doors, a figure appeared and then a second, third, and fourth. Yes, they all had found the house. I opened the gate, and the two cars pulled up to the front door. They had a tractor-trailer's worth of luggage. We formed a luggage brigade and unloaded the cars. The rest of the guests were not due to arrive until tomorrow. After everyone chose a bedroom, we sat down to wine and cheese. The conversation turned to how to help lost souls find the house. A new plan developed. We would make a larger sign and find larger balloons. The problem with the balloons, however, was that they popped when they brushed up against the tree trunks to which they were attached. One option was to leave a car at the end of the driveway with a sign: "If you are looking for Giovanna, come this way." We all knew this was merely a form of entertaining ourselves, so we continued to enjoy our evening.

Morning arrived. It was time to meet Pietro at the train. I left a map for the sleepy travelers, guiding them to the café in town. While on the way to meet Pietro, I received a call from Robert. He had landed and was in Termini. Where he anticipated connecting for the train to Chiusi After meeting Pietro, we drove to Chiusi. Robert was standing at the front of the station with a group of students. He stood out like a sore thumb, as he was approximately one foot taller than anyone around him. I jumped out, apologizing for our tardiness. Pietro and I had rescued another guest.

We found the house alive with laughter, and music. I herded everyone out to the car to help unload the provisions for our repast. Robert was assigned to his room, and a quick nap was in order for the weary traveler. Pietro took over the cooking; a few of us were allowed the privilege of washing and cutting vegetables. The rest were assigned the duty of table setting and chair locating. As we prepared lunch, another two weary guests arrived. I ushered them to the remaining rooms. The kitchen vibrated with laughter, waving hands, and voices.

Pietro was in charge. Everyone helped place the food on the table. The image I remember was that of a chain of ants raiding a picnic feast. Wine was poured all around, and plates and platters were passed. As each guest arrived, the same warning was given—this was just the beginning of a Pietro lunch. After we cleared the dishes from the first course, it was time to prepare for the *secondo platto*. Once again food, plates and platters were passed.

"There is more?" someone asked.

"Yes," I replied

"How many more courses are there?" the new guest inquired.

"Three more courses."

Laughter filled the room. Everyone was offering to marry Pietro, take him home, or stay and have him cook for them forever. The afternoon slipped past. Everyone had a short nap, and then it was off to town. I took Pietro to the station. *I blessed him for his kindness and generosity and his unequaled epicurean delights.*

When I returned home, everything was cleaned and put away. The group was outside, enjoying the afternoon sun. In the olive groves, men and women were finishing this year's harvest. Shortly we would drive to town to have our early evening coffee and wine and come up with a dinner plan. Outside the house, the parking area was filled with cars. I gave the reveille call, and it was off to Cetona. Everyone jumped into his or her respective cars with maps in hand.

We descended on Cetona, walking into the piazza. Men filled the small tables, and children played a game of tag. The women were off to the side, talking of their day's activities. When everyone was seated, I took drink orders. We talked about the beauty of the countryside and that the art found even in small villages was Metropolitan Museum quality. There was a discussion as to where tomorrow's driving tour might start. I recommended some small towns that were a short distance away. Tomorrow morning everyone would journey to a desired destination. Pietro and I would remain at the house to take care of the party plans.

We decided to have one more round of drinks at the café before heading off for dinner. Robert offered to get this round, and when he returned with the drinks, he looked at me, confused. "I don't believe it!" he said. "This only cost six euros!"

"That's impossible," the group responded with laughter.

The cost of living in the Italian countryside is one-tenth of that in the United States. Another lesson learned. The sun was setting, and the cafes filled with more men, women, small children, and pets. Robert walked back into the café in search of the *bayno* (bathroom). He came back, laughing. "You are not going to believe this. There is a serious card game going on in the back room."

"What kind of card game are they playing?" Tom asked.

"I don't know. I wasn't going to ask. There are a lot of pictures on the cards. Could be Go Fish or Old Maid," he chuckled.

There always was a card game in the evening in Italy, usually in a small back room of the café—and men only. As the weather warmed, the men moved outside.

We continued our conversation and finished our libation. At the house, there was still food from lunch for those who wished to return home for an early evening. Four of us decided to have dinner at Roberto and Lou-anna's restaurant in Chiusi. The church bells sounded. It was seven o'clock. We would all return to the house and make our way from there.

The next morning was my birthday. I woke to the smell of coffee; someone had been hand-grinding beans. I walked into the kitchen and realized I best be getting things ready for the party. Within a moment, the caterer was on the intercom, asking to have the gate opened. The long procession of food, wine, plates, glassware, linens, and chairs began. I decided to get out of the way.

A note was on the table: *"Happy Birthday, Baby." We all went to town for cappuccino. Didn't want to wake you. Enjoy the coffee. Love, the birthday revelers.*

I decided to join them in town. The sun was shining and the day perfect. I arrived to see the ragged Americans gathered around three tables. It was noon, so we decided to eat lunch at the café, as the house was a beehive of activity. After lunch, we journeyed back home—it was time to put the party dresses on and begin the festivities.

The party was the best party ever, as were the birthday cakes. Yes, I had my two cakes, and I ate them too. The night slipped away. We danced until the rooster crowed.

I feel a smile coming to my face and then think back to the darkness of the meaning of a last birthday party. April 23, 1999, would be Rinny's last birthday. Rinny loved birthdays as much as my father and I did. Though she was seventeen that year, she saw no reason not to celebrate as if it was her seventh. She insisted we buy noisemakers, party hats, and balloons to fill the house in celebration of her birthday. We needed to purchase party favors for her friends, and the favors were always crazy gifts. This year she chose snow globes. Her reason—and she always had a reason—was that the year she was born, it snowed on her birthday. The guest list was long, as were the events she had planned. She drew a picture of a donkey and donkey tails for playing Pin the Tail on the Donkey. Rinny always made her birthday dinner and her birthday cake. It was what she wanted and what she had done for years. My responsibility was to provide all the ingredients. She always was a birthday purist. Her birthday had to be celebrated on her birthday, never waiting for a weekend. I can still see her with her party hat, noisemaker and Hawaiian shirt, one finger in her ear and a smile on her face. *Happy Birthday, my love, and thank you for your brief time with us.*

With age and time, these images have become a distant memory. Yet the memories tie me to Olivetta and the hope of life and family. The celebration of life here brings me home. I always seem to be at home here, home in the sense of childhood and adulthood. I hope I honor these traditions for eternity. It is truly about the celebration, the endless toast—*salute.* One might think this life was a Bacchanalian party, and in a sense it was.

The first New Year's Eve here in Italy was quite different from my previous experiences. The saviors of the house restoration, Sarah and Pietro, had rushed to fill the house with a minimal amount of furnishing, whatever was needed for a night's sleep. There was the two-hundred-year-old bed that Sarah had bartered for me, a small lamp from their Murano shop, an espresso pot, bottles of water, candles, some flowers, and, of course, a bottle of wine. They worked so hard to welcome us. I was with Robert; it was my fiftieth birthday party that brought our lives together. He arrived early that morning from New York and took the train up to Chiusi, where we met. It wasn't cold; it was just windy. The house, only just having had its heat turned on, was damp. The windows dripped with condensation, and the fireplaces were not yet finished, but Robert would make it functional. We decided on an early dinner in Chiusi, at our friend Roberto's restaurant. As always with Roberto and Lou-anna, the greeting was warm. We laughed, hugged, and were shown our table. Dinner here always was special—it's family, it's friends, and it's home. We always waited in anticipation of Roberto's choices and pairing of food with wine. This was a gift—New Year's in Italy with our friends. Could it be any more wonderful?

Full with Italy's best wine and food, we left the restaurant. The smell of burning firewood and holiday lights draped across the streets welcomed us. People were gathered all around. We walked up the main *strada,* street and realized that the smell of firewood was not coming from inside the homes but from an enormous bonfire that had been placed in front of the Etruscan museum. The entire town gathered around the fire. Voices, songs, laughter, and music filled the air. The opera of life again appeared before us. Small children, teens, adults, and grandparents made up the aria. Large shadows were cast upon the ancient walls. A small boy ran up to us. He had been lighting firecrackers. Robert asked if he might purchase some. The child smiled and handed Robert a handful of firecrackers and then the magic igniter. A simple piece of flint would change the dynamics of this gift. The child demonstrated the proper procedure for ignition. His grandparents looked on proudly. Robert set off his first Italian firecracker. The New Year was underway. We lingered for a few more moments, thanking the small boy and his grandparents. The large bonfire was warm and filled the square with a golden glow. There was a joy in celebrating together, of sharing the beginning of a new year. We warmed ourselves and then headed back to the car.

The drive home was wonderful; all the towns had their holiday lights on. It was not quite midnight, but we were tired. The night air was cool, and the stars were as magnificent as ever. We arrived home, and Robert decided to ignite his treasure of firecrackers. However, Robert failed to toss one little firecracker, and it exploded at our feet. The house shuddered. The sound was deafening as it vibrated throughout the stone walls. We laughed. Robert continued his mini-explosion show.

The day had been perfect. We turned on the Three Tenors and allowed opera to lull us to sleep. The church bells tolled the welcoming of the New Year, breaking the stillness of the night. Church bells normally did not ring this late at night. A flash came from the window; then another flash filled the room with light. We climbed from the bed to view one of the wonders of the countryside. The villages surrounding the farmland were illuminated, each taking its turn to display its fireworks—a welcome to the New Year. It was as if a conductor had arranged this vision, one village more beautiful than the previous. Shortly after the villages began their display, each farmhouse offered a personalized version of hope, joy, and the New Year. The night sky was saturated by fireworks, The countryside was alive with the sounds of church bells and the beauty of the lights. How could one miss this? How could one not experience anything so simple and beautiful? Always grateful for the gift, we retired to bed with the anticipation of a new year. The Three Tenors still played. I looked out as the last glow of fireworks faded. The first bells of the New Year were silent.

The evening church bells ring and bring me back to today, to the small terrace where I sit overlooking the fields. I remember Sarah saying the view reminded her of Cape Cod at night, with the dark field and the small town lights illuminated in the hills. The fields, she thought, looked like the harbor. In this early twilight, I am at peace.

Chapter 7
Twilight

I had planned on a trip to town for dinner, but I feel ready for a quiet night at home, embraced by the warmth and love of the countryside. An early evening to bed will set my biological clock for the morning. Rose will have me up working early.

I have cheese and wine that I purchased this afternoon, and Rose left some homemade pasta in the kitchen. I'll make dinner and enjoy my solitude. The sounds during this gentle twilight are operatic. Birds search for their evening roost. The town rooster will make his last call of the day. I know the owl will begin his search for food soon, gliding over the fields, looking for an unaware creature. The voice of the wind as it gently brushes the olive branches adds to the opera. There is always a breeze at the end of the day. This is a signal to the world of the turning from day to night.

The pasta reminds me of the many times Uncle Nick came to make pasta at our home. It was a weekly event. He had his pasta-rolling table and a long dowel, once a wooden dowel but eventually replaced by a Lucite one. My cousin started one of the first plastic factories in the United States, and knowing the importance of a good, solid pasta roller, he designed one specifically for Uncle Nick (though it took three or four years before Uncle Nick would surrender his long-tested wooden one).

He made the knife he used to cut the pasta. It was as primitive as a Viking knife—a long steel shaft, two pieces of wood as a handle, and two bolts holding everything together. It would rust; he would sharpen and oil it. Most important, no one ever was allowed to use this sacred knife. It was Uncle Nick's alone and solely for the cutting of the pasta.

To Nick, making pasta was an afternoon event. On the table was the large volcano of flour with eggs resting in the center, waiting for his hands. It seemed like he would knead the mixture for hours. He encouraged us to practice the art of kneading, yet our hands were tiny and certainly weak. If our attempts were successful, a stick of gum would appear out of his vest pocket. There also was a shot of whiskey for Nick, that went along with the completion of the kneading process—there was an hour after completing the kneading before the rolling and cutting would take place.

We would sit together—Uncle Nick with his shot and we kids in anticipation of another stick of gum. The wait time for rolling the pasta was never really monitored—it was when Uncle Nick finished his shot and had poured a second. Rolling pasta is an art. The dough must be rolled in a perfect circle, with the same thickness throughout. Uncle Nick's rolled dough was a yard in diameter. When Nick was satisfied with the dough's thickness and size, the fun would begin. We were allowed to roll the pasta. Starting at one side, we rolled the dough toward the center, making a tube. Then we rolled the other side to the center, making a second tube. Uncle Nick then began cutting tight slices along the two rolled tubes. When the first six inches had been cut, he would slide the knife under the roll, gradually raising it. As he did this, the pasta unrolled, and formed long strings of linguine. He removed it from the knife and gently tapped us on the face with the long strings, to finish the process. We laughed with delight.

As I pick the pasta up to place it in the boiling water, I understand the importance of life here—making do with what one has. As the pasta boils, I go out to pick some herbs from the plants Rose helped me plant. The peppery olive oil from last year's harvest will be the base of the country pasta sauce. I realize that there are no understandings as to why some Italian men cook while others do not. It's something I will have to look into. One thing I do know is that when Italian men cook, the product is a gift.

I wait for the sauce to simmer and the pasta to finish. I will prepare a small salad and plate of cheese. Though dining alone always seems strange, I never really feel alone here. I came to Italy alone for many years and would dine out exclusively during that time. It allowed me the ability to meet my neighbors and to discover new recipes and friends. It has been only in the last two and a half years that I have traveled with Robert. He has become my soul mate; his love for Italy is matched only by mine. Not a moment is wasted here. Time will not be measured, not in Italy. We are like two small children, waiting to open Christmas presents. Arriving in Roma, we drive up to Villastrada. It takes just under two hours, and the minute we turn onto the Chiusi exit, we are home. I smile at this bond we have forged, grateful that an Irishman has left the boiled meats and potatoes for the lush palate of Italy.

There is a knock at the door. I hear *"Permesso?"* ("May I come in?") It is Sonya, Rose and Stefano's daughter. She wants to know if I would like to have dinner with the family tonight. I thank her but show her my work in progress. She asks if I will come for *dolce.* Of course, I will come. *Dolce* at their house is fantastic. It is like being at a *dolce* buffet. The time to arrive is 8:40 p.m. That may seem strange, but Italians use all minutes in the hour. Americans will use the hour or half hour as a designated time. Italians love the ten after, twenty to, or any small minute amount of an hour. I believe it is truly because time does not really matter, and no one is ever on time. They are on Italian time, which is any moment within an American thirty minutes. You are never half an hour late. If you say 8:40

and show up at 9:20, you are on time. Things just take a little longer here.

I offer Sonya a glass of wine and some cheese and ask if she would like to stay while I cook to keep me company. Sonya speaks no English, and as I have said, my Italian is a work in progress, but for some reason we understand each other perfectly. Sonya is beautiful and full of life. In fact, she is the perfect example of a young Italian woman, who sings, dances, loves, and embraces the land around her. She cannot stay. She must go home and help Rose with dinner. We kiss, and off she goes.

I put the finishing touches on my plate and return to the small table and chair on the upper terrace. Serenity and peace are around me. The lingering scent of the olive wood fires fills the air.

The pasta is perfect. Each bite brings a thought, a memory, and a future dream. The thought of girls' night in the country with Sarah and Zara brings a smile. An evening in the country with them is not to be missed. Sarah will visit from time to time with Zara, her trusted family pet—a beagle. We always start with a fantastic lunch, a siesta, and a walk through town. Zara loves coming to the country and has just recently discovered the multispecies pen in my neighbor's yard. For a beagle, this is a dream come true, though I'm sure my neighbor and the chickens, rabbits, and goats see it in an entirely different light. I think of last year, when they came down to celebrate my birthday.

I was alone, and Sarah had time away from the store. She arrived with pans of food and the most incredible box of pastries imaginable. She explained that she had gone to Castiglione del Lago and inquired where to find a *panificio* (bakery) and was given directions out to the country.

"They kept telling me to go out to the country, and it would be behind the cement factory. I have never seen a cement factory on the road to your house. I never saw any signs of a *panificio*. I was driving and turned down a road. I didn't see anything I was given as a landmark, but I did see a car coming toward me. I stopped, lowered my window, and asked where the pastry shop was. I got directions and found the building that looked like it was pulled from southern France—definitely not something from an Umbrian countryside. You wouldn't believe it—people were sitting outside at tables with linens and bouquets of flowers, and there even was a purple velvet rope around the tables to keep the cars at a distance. But that's not all, when you walk in, it's fantastic. The displays rival any you would find in Paris or Roma. The choices are endless but so was the line. It took me thirty minutes just to place my order. We have to go there sometime in the afternoon and have wine and a treat. I just can't believe."

We moved on, preparing lunch. After a wonderful two-hour repast, we decided to go for a walk to town and have an espresso. We left Zara at home.

The stroll was invigorating, and we met everyone I knew in town on the way. We sat out under the pergola and looked down at the farm fields and Olivetta. After an espresso, we decided to stop at the market to pick up anything we might need for dinner before continuing home and starting a fire for the evening. On the way, we picked a couple of *cachi,* from my neighbor's tree, a fruit which resembles a cross between a tomato and an orange.

"Sarah, everyone has one of these trees. I see the fruit for sale in the market, but I have never seen anyone even attempt to eat them. What is the story behind the cachi?"

Sarah laughs. "They have a funny taste, and their texture is really strange. Most of the time, people don't even pick them."

"So why did we just pick two of them?"

She looks at me with that smile and says, "I wanted you to try it. See if it makes you sick or if you like it."

We both burst out laughing. The walk always was shorter than we wished, and we soon arrived home. We opened the door, only to find the refrigerator open and the box of deluxe, luxurious pastries on the floor—empty, I might add. We looked at each other and had the same thought—Zara. We walked through the kitchen to find Zara lying on the sofa in a sugar and chocolate coma.

"I can't believe she is not dead, and I can't believe she opened that refrigerator door," Sarah said. "I think I'd better get her outside in case she gets sick."

I look up from rolling on the floor with laughter. "I'll clean up what's left of our birthday pastry treats."

With everything clean, we moved on to our evening. We talked about the farm, the land, families, politics, and friends. We drank wine—more than we should have, but we were at peace in the country. She was our guardian. When she felt we had been up too late or overly enjoying ourselves, she'd grab a piece of firewood from the stack in the living room, bring it upstairs to my bedroom, and jump up on my bed. For Zara, when the time was right, it should be lights out.

Zara dropped the log on the tile floor. When we ignored her, she brought the log up on the bed and again dropped it to the floor. We found this humorous and continued our conversation. By the fourth time, when we didn't heed Zara's call to sleep, she began to bark that beagle bark. It was at that point all lights must be out. Otherwise, she would run downstairs and look at us indignantly, as if we were deaf. Zara slept downstairs in the largest bed. She decided this on her first visit to the country. It was Zara's room and Zara's bed, and she intended to get some sleep. We laughed and granted her request, though Sarah and I continued on for a while longer. Zara soon fell asleep and dreamed, no doubt, of chasing my neighbor's chickens or at least attempting to get into their pen.

If this beagle didn't get a chicken, she was guaranteed to catch at least five little geckos or their Italian cousins. It was humorous to watch, but I always was mortified when she grabbed the little creature in her mouth, and its tail fell to the ground and continued to wiggle. Here was when I begged Sarah to please put it outside.

"You are in the Italian countryside, Sarah said. "What's a little gecko tail to you?"

Holding back the involuntary desire to vomit, I looked at her and replied, "I'll take a scorpion over those little wiggly things any day of the week. They're much slower and remind me of baby lobsters. The disengaged moving piece of an animal is more than I can bear. I like looking at animals with all their parts attached."

Sarah "You're kidding."

I regained my composure and broke out laughing. "Certainly not, remember the scorpion last night? It is just a baby lobster to me."

The thought of this wonderful life and these friends makes me smile. I am not alone, even when I am alone. The breezes become the gentle touch of a lover; the stars glisten and call me forth. The music lifts my soul, and I share it with all those before me and all those who will follow.

I think of Rinny; today is her birthday. Looking out over the fields, I am filled with joy, having shared my life with such a beautiful and strong-willed spirit. *Happy Birthday, Rinny, I love you.* Laughing, I think back to the fond memory of my two Italian birthday parties. There is nothing greater for me than the joy of sharing this wonderful land and peoples with my old friends and new neighbors. I am often reminded of those who stood on this ground before me. To those who changed the texture and landscape of this beautiful country, I am eternally grateful. I hear music again coming from the town. It is opera, and it is spectacular. I close my eyes and see with my ears and nose. Beauty fills my soul. The impish thought sits on my shoulder. I am comfortable; thoughts appear when the moment is right. The church bells ring. I must begin my journey to Rose and Stefano's.

I look for a bottle of Vin Santo to take to Rose and

Stefano's—the perfect dessert wine. The evening air has chilled a bit, and I take my scarf and jacket for the walk up the driveway. The main street is quiet. Everyone is having dinner. Then Lula, the foolish little dog, barks from the rooftop. "*Basta*," (Stop, enough). I implore her to stop. I do not want anything to break the silence of this night. She contemplates the command for a moment but continues. All the shutters are closed on the houses that line the street, and no light is emitted from the town's façade, which conceals the joy and life that is lived at this moment. It protects those inside, keeping them safe and at peace. I arrive at Rose and Stefano's and ring the doorbell.

Rose opens the window of their second-floor apartment, calling, "*Ciao! Buona sera*, Giovanna."

I hear Rose's steps coming down the stone staircase. The next sound is the click of the lock as the old wooden door opens.

The entry is dark; the aroma of dinner just enjoyed lingers in the stairwell. We walk upstairs and enter the apartment. As we enter, I see the fireplace is lit, casting an amber light across the marble foyer floor. Stefano and his brother are at the table. Sonya moves around it, finishing the *secondo piatto* cleanup, making room for *formaggio* and *dolce*. I present Stefano with the Vin Santo. He is most appreciative and places the bottle on the table. Rose vanishes to the kitchen to prepare the balance of the evening's epicurean delight. We talk about the day and the work in the fields. Stefano says it will take another four or five days to finish pruning the olive trees and that he will start on Monday. (Tomorrow is Sunday, and he will not be working.) Stefano's elder brother no longer works in the fields. Often, he will have dinner with Stefano and Rose. The brothers look identical, being separated by only two or three years. The image is of a younger and older—time-lapse photography.

Rose returns from the kitchen with the cheese plate and some fruit. Rose has questions. When I am invited to their house for dinner or *dolce*, there are always questions. I have brought my English-Italian dictionary, so I will be able to answer all questions. Rose only asks questions that she then will immediately answer herself. She has no real need for my answer. Rose begins her instructions on caring for the plants and fruit tree we have planted.

"Giovanna, they must be watered late in the day. They should never be watered in the bright sunlight!"

"I will do the watering and it will take place exactly at the same time every day. Rose will you tend them when I am gone, until they take hold?" my humble request.

"Si, Giovanna, I will do what is necessary. The plants will be safe".

Stefano breaks in. "The olive harvest may be poor this fall. The weather has not been well for trees. It has been too dry. Giovanna, you should be prepared for a weak harvest.

I am surprised Rose has allowed Stefano to speak. Normally, it is only after Rose has her agenda is Stefano allowed to speak or answer questions.

Rose regains control of the conversation. "Giovanna, Stefano has had problems with his knees. He will have to undergo surgery, and though the doctors say he should be able to work in the fall, there is a chance he will not be able to help with the olive harvest. Also, Giovanna if Stefano is not well, I will have to care for him and will not be able to help with the harvest. Sonya is only available on Sunday and Monday."

I am concerned for Stefano. He is not young and undergoing surgery is always a risk.

"Stefano, please do not worry, I am worried for you. I will make sure the trees are taken care of. You will be proud of me."

"Giovanna, I will be fine."

Now, while I profess this to both, I know in my heart that I have never attempted a harvest on my own or even as the lead. Thoughts swirl through my head. *Who can help? What can I do to make this work?*

I realize Rose and Stefano have been working at trimming the olive trees, so I ask.

"Stefano are you in pain when doing that work on the olive trees? I know it is not easy to climb up into the trees. I have watched you and Rose do the work."

It is with Italian pride he responds.

"Giovanna, it is fine. You do not have to worry."

I realize the grass underneath the trees needs to be mowed, and it is obvious that Stefano is not capable of the task. My first question to both is:

"Do you know if anyone can mow under the fields?" Without missing a breath, Stefano replies.

"Si, I will call him tonight, he will be here tomorrow or the next day, the grass will be cut. Giovanna, do not worry."

Rose clears the cheese. She declines my help, as always, saying, "*Grazie, non.*" In an Italian home, guests are not allowed to provide assistance. I always offer, though. Sarah has told me point-blank, "Get out of my kitchen. No one works in my kitchen." The sacred ground of the home is the kitchen; this is not to be forgotten. I oblige.

Although I am as full as I can imagine from my dinner, I know the *dolce* will be spectacular. The *dolce* buffet begins with no obvious end in sight. The mantra of the Italians is always "*Man, mano, man, mano.*" The conversation continues with Rose in charge. She starts with the additional work needed on the farmhouse. It needs to be painted. I have the only white farmhouse in the countryside, and this is not proper. Everyone in town refers to Olivetta as the *casa bianchi*—white house. Rose point-blank informs me this is not good. Painting a farmhouse on the Tuscan/Umbria border is not just a matter of picking a color and then finding a painter. It is an official matter; the commune must be notified by the techno's office. The official then must travel out to my house. When he arrives, he will apply three paint-color patches to the side of my house. (The commune decides which color options I have.) When I choose one of the three colors, the techno will notify the commune. It is then that I will be permitted to hire a painter to paint. It's not simple, but it preserves the beauty of the countryside. No blue chalets around here. I inform Rose that I have notified the techno and am waiting for the commune to give me guidance. A smile comes over her face, the smile I love. Her hands race to her face, and I am again in good graces with Rose. We laugh; I have passed yet another homeowner's challenge.

It is time for *caffe*, the signal we are about to end our *dolce* hour. It is an hour or longer, but an hour is the minimum required for this course. Sonya is going to meet some friends and asks if I wish to join them. I hesitate and respectfully decline, saying I have just arrived and must get some sleep tonight. She finishes clearing the table and offers me a ride home. I thank her but assure her that after all the *dolce*, I need to walk. We leave together; I kiss and thank Rose, Stefano, and Stefano's brother a good night. As we walk down the stairs, Sonya asks if maybe tomorrow evening we can have pizza together at the café. We will talk tomorrow. It is time now for *baci e buona serata,* (kisses and goodnight). We are off on our separate ways.

I decide to walk home through Gina's yard, hoping to prevent the howling rooftop guard dog from waking the entire village. The walk is refreshing; the lights of the sky and land blend. Are the stars a reflection of the lights in this imaginary harbor? Yes, at this moment, each is an expression of the other on a surface of imaginary water. The beauty of the countryside shines. The night sky is black. Small jewels light the darkness. The church bells ring, soon to be silenced by the lateness of the night.

In my contentment, I think of my children and how they are now grown. I laugh, remembering when I said to my son, "You are an uncle now."

He laughed and said, "You know what is really funny is that you are a grandmother now."

I think, *I am a grandmother. I am a grandmother. How is this possible? My children are aunts and an uncle, and I*

107

am a grandmother. I look up at the night, and think of what profound knowledge I may have provided them. I think about the unconditional love my father shared with my son. I am almost envious. When I grew up, my father worked. We had great moments—the weekly trip to the department store on the island to pick out just the right gift or, as I grew older, accompanying him and his friends on a social outing, much to the annoyance of my mother.

Tyrus, my son, shared something so special with my father that I am sure the young man Tyrus grew into was strictly a result of the love the two shared. It is their kindness, generosity, and caring that shines above all. It is a marvel to me.

I think of the time when my grown children, except for Zoe, came over to Italy for the holidays. Everyone seemed to step back in time, and they became children again. Their laughter and taunting filled the house. The stories of their childhood are now part of the walls of this home. I wait for the time when my grandson is old enough to come and spend a summer with me, to feel the joy of being a child in a country that cherishes childhood and life. To learn the life of an Italian is a sacred gift, open to the accepting. The ability to walk in the memory of generations and bring new hope and life is my reward. I patiently await my daughter Zoe's first arrival. That day will come, I am sure.

I linger just a moment longer outside to thank the souls and spirits that have given me such joy here. I'm not sure where I would be, had I not returned to Italy.

I think of Anna, my daughter, and her husband, Louis, when they came to Italy for the very first time. I promised all of my children that I would personally take them to Popoli, my grandfather's hometown. I journeyed there ten years ago, my first trip back there. It was now time for me to take my oldest daughter there.

The drive into town took us along the river on the right and the steep mountains on the left. It is almost as if we were in a storybook. High in the mountains there is a beautiful old church that looks down over the town. I knew that there was one hotel in town. We reached the center of town. Its monument in the town square is a testament to those children who fell during World War II. It was market day, and vendors lined the streets, selling fresh produce, meats, cheeses, plants, clothing, and housewares. We went to the town hall to collect original birth and marriage documents of my grandparents. I stopped to ask a small man if he might know where the *commune* building was. He not only knew but said he would take us to the building. I explained who my grandparents were and that they had been born and married in Popoli and had their first child here. This small bit of information was all that was needed. The town opened up to me. With great excitement, our new friend walked into the commune building and without hesitation, he informed the young woman as to what I needed and who I was. He told her that any help she could offer would be greatly appreciated. I provided her with dates and names. I thought this process would take two weeks at best and cost a small inheritance, but to my astonishment, the woman said that I could pick the information up the next morning. I wanted to jump over the counter and kiss her. With this major quest underway, it was time to enjoy the churches and monuments of Popoli.

We walked down the streets. The smell of fresh herbs and cooking meats filled the air. The sun was shining, and the town was so alive. Everyone was bartering for a better price, the next great deal of the week. The beauty of these small town markets usually held once a week was that no one paid the asking price. The vendors understood this, however, and always added a little on to the original price to account for the bartering, a novel way for everyone to believe he or she got a fantastic deal, while the vendor was assured a profit.

We crossed the small bridge in town and walked down along the river. This was the river Uncle Nick always talked about, telling us tales of its power and productivity. Looking down at the river, it made little sense. What was so compelling about this tiny river? Maybe Uncle Nick thought it was a big river because he was small at the time. We walked farther up and to my dismay, I saw this must have been a raging river at one time, but a power plant had been added. Though now not functioning, it basically had dammed the river. Now, instead of turning turbines for power, the water raced through canals and back down into itself. The sound was amazing. The water sprayed on to the street. What a river. We continued our walk and realized that the town had been extensively bombed during the World War II. The train station and residential areas were mere shadows of a former life, a former home.

We decided to look for the cemetery. I was here a long time ago, and I was unfamiliar with the exact directions. We walked into the local bank, thinking someone there must have a small understanding of English, as my Italian certainly would not get me through the cemetery search. I began to speak to the bank teller. The gentleman behind me did speak English. He introduced himself—his name was Paulo—and he agreed to take us to the cemetery. Kindness, in Italy, extends everywhere to everyone.

Paulo drove us back over the bridge and out into the countryside for what seemed to be twenty minutes, but I was sure it was more a result of my anticipation of arriving and looking for lost relatives. We pulled up a small road, and in front of us was a large stone building with a wrought-iron gate. Off to the side was a small house. After we parked, Paulo walked us over to where the cemetery keepers had their office. Without realizing where we were going or who we would meet, we blindly followed. *Permesso*, ciao, (hello, may I come in) the first man appeared. He was the tallest Italian I had ever seen. Next came the shortest and stoutest. For a moment, it was hard to contain my reflex action of wanting to laugh. The men began talking, hands moving up and down. I was not sure if this was going as well as I had hoped. Within a few moments, Paulo, waved us over and explained that the two men would retrieve the cemetery records dating from the mid-1800s. I knew this would be a way of tracking my grandparents and great-grandparents. They motioned us to enter and sit down at a small table. On the table sat the books. They were simple and all handwritten in beautiful script. I started at the beginning. The town was small and the number of entries few. I found my great-grandmother, but I would need to verify this with the birth certificate information tomorrow. I also understood that my grandfather's brother had returned to Popoli from America in the early 1900s. What I didn't know—and what I didn't expect to find out and still cannot truly fathom—was that in March 1944, within the short period of three days, hundreds of Popoli's citizens died, including my grandfather's brother Peter and his entire family.

Paulo was still speaking with the caretakers. With tears in my eyes, I begged him to tell me what had happened here and where they all were buried. Paulo asked the two caretakers about the cause. Such a look appeared on the men's faces that I knew nothing good would come from this. The town had been bombed. It was three days of bombing, and the town was shattered. Entire families were killed, young and old alike. The train station was one of the many targets at the time. Paulo asked where I might find their remains. The men's faces became sorrowful, and then they tossed their arms and legs, looked at Paulo, and said that there was very little left of their bodies. Most were placed in a common grave. The town's monument was a monument to everyone who died during those raids. This was not what I wanted to hear; this could not have been what happened to this beautiful country, to my family. I stood there looking at my daughter, our eyes laden with tears, as the two caretakers came over and wrapped their arms around us. The pain of war, the stains on the earth, of young and old, lived in their hearts and souls. Regaining some composure, we asked if we might walk through the cemetery to honor those who had lived here. They escorted us to the gate. The marble-faced tombs with histories and photographs told of the life of this town and of those who were here; seeing more than most should ever have to see. We walked to where many members from my grandmother's family now rested. The flowers lined the face stones, candles flickered, and lives were honored. Paulo stayed with us and said that my grandmother's family was very large and important in Popoli and that he would like to arrange for us to meet a relative who owned a market in town. I thanked him and the two caretakers for all their help and compassion. We followed Paulo down to town. We talked little on the drive back to town, as if a long, silent moment of prayer could remove the past suffering and pain. At five o'clock, we would meet in town at the central café.

Anna and Louis were stunned by the history and pain that they had just witnessed. I could hardly wait for the afternoon to end. The anticipation of meeting my grandmother's relatives was paramount. The hotel was nearby. We parked and checked in. As we began our walk through the streets, we saw the extensive damage—entire buildings with just the door frame left, as if they were the monuments to those who had lost their lives during the war. Anna and Louis could not imagine this devastation. War, to them, was something their grandfathers might talk about or something that was made into a movie. Their generation did not suffer "war," one of the few generations that managed to make it to young adulthood without knowing the horrors of war, except on TV or in the movies. I realized how hard it was for them. I knew how hard it was for me.

It was time to sit and just look at the beauty around us. Emotionally, there was little left in us. We walked to the café. The sun was low in the sky, and clouds danced in front of the sun, creating shadow patterns on the walls. The central monument now had new meaning, one step closer to us than we had thought, but we were at my family's home, and there was reason to rejoice. Soon, we would meet our relative. We ordered coffee and then a glass of wine. The waiter brought out a beautiful assortment of antipasto. Louis and Anna wanted to continue to walk through town and explore. I was not sure if they just needed time to digest all that had happened in a brief few hours, or if they really wanted to do a little shopping. I was glad to have a few moments alone with my emotions and thoughts and lost relatives. The local men filled the outside seats of the café; time to begin the daily card game. The game always took place with a juice glass of wine, picture cards, and cigarettes. The entire world was right again. *Pace*, (Peace) is home in Italy. One of my favorite parts of this time of the day was when the town elderly came out for the constitutional walk. I loved watching the women, with their hair perfect, wearing what most individuals today would call their "Sunday best." They walked with elegance, an air of contentment and peace, never rushing, stopping to talk with children and mothers. Usually, they were accompanied either by their daughters or granddaughters. Seldom did I see an elderly man accompany them. The elderly men seemed to have found comfort and solace in their card games and their compatriots, dressed in their button-up vests, jackets, small ties, fedoras, and classic Italian pants. My mind gradually found a sense of peace; my emotions were soothed by the gentle kindness that surrounded me.

Anna and Louis returned. They had walked back over to the ruins near the train station. Louis said it was as if Italians never wanted to forget what war can do, and as they protected their art and architecture, they honored the horrors so as not to relive them. I agreed. It was one thing to watch destruction on TV, but it was completely different to face it every morning on your way to the market, café, or work. Paulo arrived, and with him was a middle-aged woman—she was the widow of my grandmother's sister's grandson. We sat down with wine and antipasto, as she explained that there were other relatives in town, but she was unable to contact them on such short notice. I asked for any stories she might remember of the time before my grandparents left for America. She only knew that they left before she was born. Having married into the family, she did not know all that had happened earlier. Her husband had died prematurely, and she now ran their market. She had not lived through the war but knew from her parents' stories that many people from the town had perished. So many families lost everyone. After the war, many of the town's residents decided to move to America. It was hard in Popoli after the war. There was so much destruction and so little work or food.

She said she could not stay long but invited us to her house for dinner the following night, when she would prepare a proper meal. With Paulo translating for me, I thanked her but explained that we had to leave in the morning. I said we would love to come back and see her another time. I thanked her for taking the time to meet us and for her kind invitation.

We decided to return to the hotel, go out for an early dinner, and retire early. Morning led us to the *commune* and the documents that should confirm our heritage. The *commune* opened at ten o'clock, giving us time to have a café and pastry. When we arrived, the woman was pleased to see us. She had all the documents ready, stamped with the town seal to certify they were authentic. I asked what the charge was for the work.

She said, "One euro. The euro is for the seals."

I was in a state of disbelief. If I had asked for similar documents in the States, it might have cost one hundred dollars and taken three weeks to get the documents. "That is such a small amount," I said. "Are you sure it is not more?"

She assured me that was the entire amount required for the documents. We smiled, gathered our documents, and walked out into the sun-filled morning. As we walked to the car, I saw a man who looked exactly like Uncle Nick—same manner of dress, same face, same size. Then I remembered that Uncle Nick was from Popoli. I asked the man if he was related to my uncle's family—he was. Anna became so excited, she said, "Show him the papers! Show him the papers."

I took out the treasured documents for him to read. When

he finished, he called two other men over, and they also read the documents. Anna took photographs. Before long, there were six men, all looking a lot like Uncle Nick, looking at the papers. I explained we had arrived to find more information on my father's family and that my aunt had married a man from Popoli. It was confirmed—there were more relatives. Anna took more photographs of everyone, and we exchanged mailing addresses. At this moment, for us, yesterday's horrors were now softened by today's joy. Our mission was complete. Our quest was a complete success.

I am pulled back to the early evening by the church bells. The night air has chilled. I can smell the fire inside, and I walk into the warmth and comfort of my home, my family, and my life here in the countryside.

Chapter 8
Home

The house is warm. The fire, started early in the evening, casts a subdued glow in the upper living room, and it illuminates the stairway. The scent of dinner and the fresh herbs in the kitchen are mixed into an interior garden scent. The fireplace downstairs has faded to a low glow. Time is forever an unknown companion, yet it is time to move through the evening, and I am drawn upstairs. The upstairs living room is small. It is my late-night private sanctuary when I am here alone. The fireplace creates a cozy feel, and its burnt okra hue visually adds warmth to the room. Not quite ready for sleep, I place two more logs on the fire. Here, my thoughts come together. In the solitude of the night, meanings reveal themselves to me. I turn on a Gregorian chant, and the fire crackles as the past and the present merge. I completely enjoy this wonderful music when I'm alone or when I am in Assisi to visit St. Francis's tomb. St. Francis is one of my most admired saints. I have traveled to many of his special places that crisscross Italy. I once came across a book called *On the Road with Saint Francis of Assisi*, a work of dedication and proven enlightenment. The book retraces the steps of this thirteenth-century saint. After reading it, I realized that of all the areas of Italy I might have chosen, the one that attracted me most is the one where St. Francis spent most of his religious search for enlightenment. Olivetta is not far from his miracle of the stigmata at La Verna.

La Verna is truly the spiritual center for anyone following St. Francis. His soul walks through the forest and is carried with the wind. The small monastery there provides meals and shelter for those who wish to spend the night in the woods of St. Francis. The cave of the stigmata and the stone pathway where he fought the devil remain untouched. La Verna is where St. Francis walks today. Assisi is a religious mecca, the site of Roman temples covered by Christian temples and then rediscovered Roman temples, unearthed and exposed in the bowels of the recent churches. During the cooler months, the dampness of the church enters your body; the sunlight blesses you. Only a few modern conveniences have been added—a light here, a speaker there. I never really noticed the public address system until one day a voice spoke over it, saying, *"Silenco."* This is a religious building, still in use for religious purposes, and it's due the proper respect. The most wondrous gift is walking into St. Francis's tomb while a mass is in progress. The voice of the priest and the cascading sounds of the congregation as they sing always bring tears of joy and hope.

Robert and I traveled with a friend to visit Assisi. We made the thirty-minute drive around Lago Trasimeno and then on to Assisi. We entered the basilica and walked to the entrance of St. Francis's tomb. As we walked down the worn stone stairway, I heard what I had never heard before in the tomb—a Franciscan father was singing mass. Robert and I looked at each other. I looked at my friend Paul. "This is a blessing," I whispered. The tomb's chapel was small and darkly illuminated with a soft emphasis on the massive stone tower that entombed St. Francis. Nothing was ever as spiritually moving to me. I had dreamed of such a time when I could attend mass and receive communion in this sacred spot. We sat down in the narrow, simple wooden pews and prayed. The mass of the entire basilica was supported with one major beam holding the sacred remains of St. Francis.

St. Francis was literally the spiritual pillar of this artistic wonder. I had the strength of everyone who had prayed and asked for blessing in this most sacred chapel. The candles of the chapel danced across the stone walls.

The fire crackles and snaps me back to my haven—my small country home, I sit on the large chair in front of the fire and find total peace in my own sanctuary. The writing desk is behind me and overlooks the fields. There is a picture of St. Francis, a statue of Buddha, a rosary my father carried during the World War II, and an antique book of Italy titled *Historians' History of the World*, volume IX, published in 1907. I take the book from the desk, along with a piece of paper and pen. Returning to the overstuffed chair, I begin to read. The book is filled with beautiful etchings, and for tonight, I will succumb to their beauty and leave the literary passages for when Robert arrives. Our love for this country is deep. We spend hours at night in front of the fire in winter and outside in the spring, summer, and fall, always reading. My eyes are not what they used to be, so he will read to me. This is more like an open dialogue than reading. Comments and thoughts are always added. A book can take a week or a month to read, tonight however, it is just me, and I will be content with my music and my etchings.

The day has been long. It was just this morning that I walked down the hill to board the ferry to the mainland. It was just this morning that I met an incredible air marshal, and it is this evening that has brought life to my soul. As I look through the images, I notice three folded, computer-typed pages—poems. I begin to read them.

I.　　*That which you have given*
That which you have given
Does not fall on deaf ears.
That which you have given
Is not blind
To the Light;
That moment
Lost in a moment
Of
Chaos,
Is only Dante
Or better
Clouds;
That moment
Is not lost.

It sits before me,
A longing, lost
View of past life;
It sits
Within my ears,
A lost
Voice;
It sits,
Classical;
They sit
Filling my space,
Sharing centuries of life,
Lost to stone
And hallowed voice;
Yet
You sit before me
With voice
And Life

II.   *Remembered*
       That last breath that
       Stood between you and void
       Hovers around this canyon
       Of thought
       And love
       That last breath will
       Always be my first.

III.   *Ode to knowledge*
       That book you casually laid down,
       That book with light and wisdom ... shedding darkness
       Would you imagine a thought would not move forward
       To change.
       That silent thought—
       Was it silence or awakening you sought?
       What image had befallen you?
       That book you casually laid down.
       Left its mark ... the mark ... the gift ...
       That book you laid down.

IV.   *Italia*
       At night your voice fills the darkened silent arena.
       The voice of agony—yet not
       Attributed to win or loss
       A part
       Of a long lost memory
       What silence and word
       Do you wish to unravel
       What injustice lurks beyond
       Recognition—your voice fills
       The dark silent arena.

V.   *Restless*
       Who walks across hallowed
       Grounds.
       Indifference their
       Shroud. Make way for the
       Injustice accepted and hover.
       Who walks across hollowed
       Ground.

VI.   *Homage to Williams'*
       Red wheelbarrow
       Others knew it
       And knew it to be
       A red wheelbarrow

VII.   *Homage to life after death's first breath*
       That first breath lays to rest the unanswered prayers
       Minions walk about
       Yet that first breath lingers
       As the voice of life or rather death
       Yet death becomes only those walking in fear
       Death becomes in the corner of your breath
       Death is your fear

VIII. *Your shadows cannot harm me*
       You cast darkness
       As clouds rollover the sun
       For me is not an entity
       Me is your imagination
       There are no shadows ...
       Light embraces the
       Soul, wisdom strength, knowledge
       You cannot harm me
       There is no me.

That which you believe comes before and after you
That which you believe is you ...
Does not exist
Exist you say yes
In your mind ...
Yet search first
For our soul ...
Lost,
Search for you ...
You do not exist.

IX.   *You cast no shadows*
Yet your image is brazen it marches
On as if in defiance of time or place
The shadows cast are those who would do you wrong,
Who would watch your fate, success,
Who now ride on its crest
The crest is not meant to be borne by those of impure
        hearts
Your shield will torture those souls
Who dare to carry it in your name.
You sought no fame or glory,
Your fame and glory came from these traits.
Your shield will continue, you will
Not cast shadows, you will only cast light.

X.   *The comfort of your souls*
Dances in my mind
Lost to the voice of
Guardian angels
Those have protected that
Which rest on the soul
Of those not martyred
Lost to the few that would
Chose to stand on the fallen
Yet not on their own souls.

XI. *Today, in thought of*
     You, both of you
     My mind raced to understand
     That moment you walked down
     The aisle carrying my daughter in
     Your hand.
     That moment is not lost

     Today, in thought of
     You, both of you
     My mind raced to understand
     That moment you walked up
     The aisle carrying my daughter in
     Your hand.
     That moment is not lost

     You have walked my
     Daughters, both up the aisle
     One up the aisle-not alone
     Yet forever I am grateful
     You will only walk one
     Of my daughters
     Down the aisle

I realize that my breath is heavy. My eyes glance over to the fire, and I am filled with serenity. I remembered writing those poems—it seems like an eternity ago. It was an eternity. I think of my children who have taught me more than anyone else. The important lessons were learning how to laugh when your heart tells you it is broken, how to cry when others suffer and you are safe, and always to remember to be grateful and gracious. I realize they are young adults, moving through their lives. They have aged. I am remembering.

I leaf through my book. The fall of Roma always intrigues me. The etching depicts a broken city, vines covering the once-pristine columns that stand majestically in the center of the city. The cell phone rings. I realize it's downstairs and off I go. "*Pronto*," Hello, I answer.

On the other end of the line is my marshal; he is coming for a visit. His plans have changed; he never made it to Termini. He and a friend will take the train to Chiusi in the morning.

Laughing, he says, "I mean, in the sense of Italian morning. We should arrive just before noon."

"Would you like the local small-town tour, a lunch on the farm, or no plans? I highly recommend the no plans."

Laughing, Mike agrees.

I will meet them in Chiusi at 11:50 a.m. *Perfecto. Ciao.*

I think of all the beautiful small towns surrounding Villastrada. Mike and his friend will be here for just the day, and I want them to enjoy the countryside.

The phone rings again. This time, it's my daughter Zoe, reminding me I was to have called to assure her I had arrived safely. I often think she is the grown-up, and I am the wandering minstrel child.

"I was worried," Zoe says. "I know today is Rinny's birthday and you are alone. So tell me if you are okay."

"I'm fine. The flight was late, but I met a federal marshal."

I could hear dead silence on the other end of the line, followed by her response: "Tell me you didn't invite him to the house, and he is either there or will be there shortly."

"He's a marshal and his plans were changed, so he and a friend are coming up tomorrow for the day."

"You are always inviting people you don't know to come and stay at the house. Are you sure he is a marshal? Did he tell you that, or did he show you some identification?" Her voice becomes maternal.

"He told me that, and that's enough for me," I protest.

"You just can't invite people you don't know to the house. What happens if they tie you up and—"

"I'll make sure he gives me his paperwork," I interrupt, "if that makes you feel any better. I'll hide any valuables, all the knives, and especially any rope I might have here." I try to assure her that I'm fine and that he is who and what he says he is. Then I add, "Besides, Rose and Stefano will be working in the grove. I'm more frightened of Rose being angry at me for not working than I am of a possibly crazed marshal."

With that, she breaks into laughter. "Okay, crazy lady, just let me know you are okay at the end of the day."

"Now tell me—how you are doing?" I ask. "Did you get to take Bingo over to see Rinny at the cemetery?"

"Gabrielle rode Sam, and I rode Bingo. It was such a beautiful day. After the cemetery, we took the horses down to the beach for a ride." Her voice begins to weaken. "I miss her."

"Rinny is always with you," I tell her, "and she owes you big time for taking care of her horse, Bingo, as well as you do. You really know she is with you when he gives you a hard time. It's Rinny's stubbornness shining through and offering you that last challenge."

I can hear her begin to laugh. "Thanks, Mom. You're right—he does act like a brat sometimes, and it must come from Rinny. I love you. Don't forget to call me tomorrow."

""Love you. How can I forget to call you? If I forget, you will come and bring me back." We laugh and the conversation is over.

I haven't slept, but I don't sleep much anyway, so I decide I'll just stay up and continue perusing the Italian history book and listening to the chants. The serenity of the night is too perfect to end. Sleeping in Italy is almost a waste of time. It's too beautiful; life is so precious. Why waste it on sleep? I remember reading somewhere that we sleep when the soul is restless. My soul is never restless here. Here in Italy, my soul is pampered with every breath, every view, and every encounter that presents itself to me. I drift back to thoughts of Rinny and her death eight years ago. I think that we as a family now take nothing for granted, that my children are so protective of me and I more than ever of them. Death rears its head at the right and wrong time. I know I must have had anger and rage in my body, but today, that has been replaced by compassion, grace, gratitude, and thanks. Rinny was, as each of my children are, a gift. Her journey on this planet was short but certainly profoundly meaningful. The old proverb that says only the good die young has solace, yet at the same time, we're all good. I also know some are more gracious than others on their path. Some people are here to learn; others are here to teach. She taught her lesson, and it was time to leave. I'm not sure why her departure was violent, but it was possibly the last lesson she taught. Violence is not always what it appears to be. Violence can be hidden in the cuddles of anything. She is here; she is with my children, and her lessons have not fallen on deaf ears. I realize today's tears are now tonight's smiles. My chants are over. It is time to embrace Rinny's birthday. I rummage through the CDs and find her copy of Smashing Pumpkins, place it in the CD player, pour a glass of wine, and celebrate Rinny's birthday. I am with her, and we are at peace.

The phone rings again.

It's Robert. His voice sounds concerned. "You didn't call. Are you all right?"

"I'm fine."

"You know I was worried. I remembered that today is Rinny's birthday, and you are alone. I took some flowers over to the cemetery and said hello to Rinny and the rest of our families and friends. It's starting to take quite some time to see everyone over there. We are getting old." The tremor in his voice deafens me.

"Robert, I'm fine. I had a few moments—you know that happens, and to be truthful, it's good it happens." I fill the conversation with my events of the day and add that I met a marshal on the plane.

Before I can finish, he asks, "Did you invite him to the farmhouse?"

"Yes," I said, knowing full well he expected nothing less of me.

"Can he come?" was his response.

"He and a friend are coming tomorrow. He was to fly back, but the plans were changed, and a friend of his is in Roma with him at the airport hotel. He just called. I think he thought I was crazy. By the end of the flight, he knew I was just *pazzo*." With that, I laugh.

"Where are you going to take them?"

"I don't have a plan, but as an Italian, I need to come up with something, so I'm thinking either lunch at the farmhouse, or lunch at Mona Lisa, or a stroll through Chiusi with lunch. It's open-ended. Zoe thinks I'm crazy, but I cherish the nickname 'crazy lady,' so I'm sticking with it. He is just a little younger than Anna. We'll be fine."

Robert knows this is the way I live life. Then he adds, "I forgot to tell you. Anna and Ty called. They wanted to let you know they are thinking about you. I told them you went to Italy, and your phone has a mind of its own, and that you might not be able to reach them. They send their love."

"Please let them know the phone only works if I get a call in. No direct dialing to the States without first a call in. Zoe has this figured out."

Robert reassures me, "I will definitely have them call you. I promise."

"Did you find out if you can help with the pruning? I know Rose is going to have me picking up rocks with a toothpick, and Stefano is not doing that well. So if there is any way you can come to help just for a few days that would be fantastic."

"I won't know until tomorrow, but when I do, I'll let you know."

"Tell everyone I love them, and let Grandma know I'm safe. I'll be safe in my haven here."

"*Perfecto*," Robert says. "You are crazy, and you just don't know how to be anything other than kind. I know you say it's what Italians do, and you are right. Enjoy." I could hear him laughing over the line. He does understand and love me.

I end the conversation the only way I know. *"Baci e sogni d'oro"*—my signature good night, kiss, and golden dreams.

I start the Smashing Pumpkins, but the phone rings again.

This time, it's Anna, her voice urgent.

"Mom, are you all right? Robert said you went to Italy, and I wanted to let you know I was thinking about you."

"Anna, I'm sorry. I am fine. As you know, being here grants me solace. I'm sorry I didn't call, but my cell phone is Italian. Unless I get an incoming call, I can't dial out to that number. Are you and Lou and little Louie okay? It's not just hard for me; I believe it's harder for you and your brother. I was sad this morning and at lunch, but tonight, I'm in Italy and Rinny is with me. In fact, Smashing Pumpkins is playing right now. I'm sure the Italians worry when the lights are on, shutters open, and fire blazing."

Anna interrupts. "Mom, I know your neighbors, and they know you are *pazi*. That's why they love you—get over it. They know you are crazy because you don't sleep, and you work your butt off. I don't believe they are worrying about the lights or music. But are you really okay?"

I sense concern in her voice. "Anna, where is the place that gives me peace? Today is a great day. Today is the day Rinny was born. She, like all of you, was a gift. Oh and just a sidebar—remember when she came home from the hospital, and you thought she was one of your dolls. You took her out of the bassinet and placed her in the closet with your dolls. Do you remember? I only realized it when she started to cry, and I couldn't find her."

"Mom, I was three! I thought she was a doll. I do remember. But I can't believe I did it." She is laughing.

"That makes two of us. I was thinking about the trip you and Louis took to discover Popoli. That was such a great trip."

Her voice fills with happiness. "That was the best trip ever."

"Anna, one reason is that both Louis and I spoiled you the whole time."

"That's what you're supposed to do. You're my mom, and Louis was my fiancé."   "I have to give Louis credit. At least I wasn't pulled into every shop throughout Italy. However, I noticed I was the one pulled into the jewelry store. As I remember clearly, I wasn't shopping. But as it turned out, I was shopping not for me but for you. That's a trait Rinny taught you all. If you believe in it, don't give in. I'll have to talk to her someday about that."

"It wasn't that bad. It was like your engagement gift to me."

"Your engagement gift was paying for your wedding. I thought that was a great gift. Or maybe it wasn't." Anna is now laughing so hard. I join in with her and then say, "I trust Hawaii is warm and wonderful. I miss you all. I think it's time we all move to Italy. I know you love being here". At this moment, my heart truly misses my children.

"Mom, we all love you. You are crazy, but we love you. Stop working so hard. You used your body, then your mind, and then your body. It's time to go back to your mind—you know what I mean."

"I know. It's just the in-between down time that takes a little transition. I promise I will." I pause, wondering if I should tell her about the marshal or keep it a secret. I know Anna so well. She will be on the phone with me until sunrise if I even mention I have invited someone I just met to the house, but only because I'm alone. So I think I'll just skip over that for the moment.

"Mom, are you there? I didn't hear you?"

"Sorry—where is my grandson? I want to talk to him."

"Nana," a faint voice comes over the phone.

"Ciao, Louie, *come sta*? What are you doing today? I miss you so much."

"Nana, we went to the beach." I can hear Anna coaxing him through the conversation. *Tell her thank you for the book,* "Nana, thank you for the book."

"Mom, he loves the book," Anna says. "Thanks. He always laughs when you talk Italian to him. I bought Maisey tapes for him to start speaking Italian."

"Anna, *perfecto.* He makes me laugh. I think he will be smarter than all of us by the time he is four. I love you and will talk to you in a couple of days. Everything here is just fine. Thank you for calling. *Baci.* I love you. Give those two handsome men a kiss for me"

"Mom, I love you."

I'm thinking I just received a get-out-of-jail card. If anyone tells Anna I invited a stranger and a stranger's friend to the house, she'll get on a plane from Hawaii, or worse yet, she will call the authorities and have them arrive with guns. At this point, however, I believe all bases are covered. The CD has finished. I decide to put on the one Gabrielle made for me of Rinny's favorite song. The phone rings again.

"*Pronto.*"

"Mom, are you okay?" Gabrielle asks. "I just talked to Robert, and he said you flew to Italy to take care of some business. I thought you were leaving tomorrow. I went to the cemetery and then to the house, and Robert said you had left for Italy. I am with him now. Is everything all right? He also said you invited—"

"Gabrielle, I am fine," I interrupt her. "Yes, I did invite Mike to the house, and he is coming with a friend. It's nothing big." At this point I think everyone is about to arrive with the *poliza.* "Promise me you will not tell Anna."

"Why?"

"You know it is because Anna always over-reacts to these things. Okay? Promise me."

"I promise. Mom, I just want to make sure you're okay. Zoe and I rode the horses to the cemetery this morning to see

Rinny and Grandpa, and I saw the flowers and couldn't reach you. Also, Robert's parents and brother had flowers. I'm sorry to call so late."

"It's not late. I don't like sleeping, as you all know. I ordered the flowers before I left. Littlest one, I am fine. I am listening to the CD you made for me from Rin's music, but I can't get past the first two songs. Are you, Zoe, and Robert going to have dinner together at the house?"

"We are going to cook at our house, and Robert is coming over. It's easier. We also want to watch the videos Rinny use to make. Remember the Beanie Baby Christmas Carol? The best one was the one she made that made fun of the talk show where all the people get on stage. Then they start screaming at each other and hitting each other. Do you remember that?"

"You mean the Jerry Springer Beanie Baby Spoof? Yeah, I remember, the one with the interspecies Beanie Babies. That is so funny. I love watching it. She was so funny."

There is a short silence on the phone before Gabrielle says, "When are you coming back?"

"Well, I thought I'd send you all a ticket, sell the house in New York, and force you to become Italian citizens. What are your thoughts on that? Maybe you can discuss them over dinner. Robert and Zoe have my itinerary. They are the grownups in the group. The rest of us are just slightly right of *pazzo*. I love you so much. I am fine. Enjoy the videos. I'll try to call tomorrow."

The thought of those videos has me laughing beyond control. Rinny was one funny girl. But more than that, she had a sharp sense of justice and expressed it through her humor. I realize I have been on the phone for quite a while, so I'd best run down to get the phone charger. The only live wire I keep while here is with my children, and that is through this small, antiquated cell phone. As I go down the stone stairway to the kitchen, I realize I am now more awake than before. I grab a bottle of water, a glass of wine, and the phone charger. The fire has retired for the night. Small coals of amber light glow their last breath. I walk back up to my haven. The fire there is roaring, and the sounds of Rinny fill the room. My solitude is now a concert of joy. She is here. The fireplace, a mainstay of our winter life, is glowing. The one missing feature is candles. It is time to replace *Historians' History of the World* with "Life of Rinny." I light the candles, place them around the room, and turn off the light. I snuggle back into the overstuffed chair and listen.

The candle flames dance across the wall. The hearth is alive with sounds of crackling wood, and a miniature firework sparks.

I return to my antique book, mesmerized by the beautiful etching. The skilled artist's hand created detail in each plate that is stunning. I realize that this book was published before my father was born but approximately at the same time my grandfather traveled to America to find an American dream for himself and his family. So much more has happened to this country since the publication of this book. My father's and daughter's entire lives were created and ended in this time span. I can't image any history without these two. I miss them terribly, and it is only the warmth and comfort of Italy and my home that now consoles me. Sleep overcomes me, and I realize it's time to retire for the day. The master bedroom is just off the second floor living room. I can watch the fire from my bed as I fall asleep. *Thank you, God, for another precious day.*

Chapter 9
Daybreak

I wake to the welcome sound of the wind rustling through the olive leaves and branches, here in the Umbrian countryside. The golden glow of the rising morning light illuminates the room. The rooster, with one vocal cord, calls out to the entire town. The church bells ring out from the brick steeple. An opera is beginning. I linger just a few moments before day begins her sweet journey for me. I slip backwards or forwards—the choice is not mine to make. The sunlight slips through the door and window of the bedroom. There are no shutters on the second floor of the casa. The luminosity of the moon at night and the sun during the day constantly fill the room with a subtle glow. I feel the sun beginning to warm me. The rooster calls out again. The slumber of the night has slipped away. My eyes open. I see the fields vibrant in color—lush greens juxtaposed with the dark brown soil. The color of the soil is a perfect Crayola crayon brown, so perfect I can almost smell it as I look out over the field. My foot touches the cold, rustic terra cotta floor, a sensation that causes my foot to recoil, and the warm linens swaddle me. I beg a moment longer to myself. Must I awake from this slumber? The wind rushes through the open door and brushes my cheeks, a gentle mother's hand attempting to encourage me to wake. I drift off, and for a few moments, I look at the bedroom walls that now surround me.

These walls, once painted white and teal, now carry the sign of their old legacy. Once they were broken, then repainted, and repainted once again. Today they stand as they stood when the *casa* was built, with the few exceptions of re-plastered channels for the new electric. I think of the deep navy blue my daughter Rinny chose to paint the walls of her bedroom. It was not so much that she wanted to paint but that she convinced me that we should paint together.

"Do you really want navy blue walls?" I'd asked.

"We are watching a movie on the Dalai Lama. Do you want to interrupt?" she responded.

"I thought we were painting. Are we painting, or are we watching a movie?" I asked.

Rinny put down her brush and said, "We are watching a movie while we are painting. It is simple. Don't you understand?"

"I understand, but what does one have to do with the other?"

"It's simple. We are painting, learning, and getting insight, all at the same time. Some people paint and listen to music. We are painting and obtaining knowledge and wisdom. Doesn't that make more sense to you?"

"I appreciate this and respect that we are painting. There is a spiritual enlightenment in the Dalai Lama's teaching, but doesn't it make more sense to watch the movie and then paint?" Rinny became annoyed at this point and looked at me with exasperation. I thought it best to change the subject and asked, "Okay, but why have you chosen such a dark blue for the entire wall?"

"Mom, it's not dark. It's blue, and it is basically the background for my design."

"What design are you talking about? Do you have a sketch for this design?"

"Mom, the sketch is in my head. Part of the reason for

watching the movie on the Dalai Lama is to gain clearer insight into my design. Now do you understand?"

"I understand even less now than I did when we began this painting project."

"Okay, you have always taught us that it doesn't matter what you call your god. God is merely the English word for something larger than us. I remember you using the example of a cat. A cat is a *cat* to us, it is a *gatto* to the Italians, and it is a *chien* to the French. No matter what word you use, it doesn't change what it is. Remember when I took Atlantis as my confirmation name?"

"Rinny, I remember all too well. In fact, to this day I am not certain why the priest didn't have a heart attack. Or even more amazing, that the church did not fall down on all of us."

"Mom, it's a name that has different meanings for everyone. It's a mythological place. We each see it for what we want to see in it. There is nothing more or less. It's like my design for this wall. You see darkness. I see a backdrop for a spiritual design that I am working on, and it is becoming clearer as I listen to this movie."

I was frustrated and began to think and talk to myself. I tried to have a greater understanding of what might be my daughter's spirituality or a con game she was playing with me so that she could paint the wall this dark blue.

"So what is your spiritual design plan?" I asked.

Rinny laughed. "What do you mean, what is my plan? My plan is right before you, and you don't understand. We are watching the history of the Dalai Lama, and I have told you my plan is spiritual and artistic. Mom, you know I am spiritual and artistic. You will see—"

"Rinny I love you, but this newfound spirituality and artistic clarity is slightly confusing. Can you help me here?"

"Mom, who do you think taught all of us this? Why do you think I'm a Catholic watching a movie on the Dalai Lama? Why do you call yourself a Catholic, Zen, and Buddhist? Don't you think that was confusing to us when you tried to explain the similarities of all these different religions? Don't you think it is confusing to our friends when they show up and there is a Buddha, Virgin Mary, crucifix, and Ganesh all standing next to each other?"

Yes, I thought, *every religion and every human has worth and value and a different language and word to go with it.* "Rinny, I must admit you're right. I'm still not sure about the navy blue wall. Can we just watch the movie and paint later?"

"Paint later? As I have been taught by you, work with your spiritual guides."

"Excuse me. This is why I love you. You are using my religion to your advantage and conning me at the same time."

"So, can you just watch the Dalai Lama and help me paint this room navy blue?" Rinny asked. "It's about our spirituality because we are all here, and I don't mean you and me. I mean we are here—your friends, my friends, and our family of souls. Now please paint, watch the movie, and don't talk."

"Okay, I won't talk."

And so we continued to paint as the late afternoon soon became early evening. I broke the silence. "Rinny, what about having to feeding the rest of the family dinner tonight? We are the two cooks in the family, and we are painting your walls and watching the history of the Dalai Lama."

"Mom, you feed us all the time, and I'm not talking just food. I'm talking about feeding us."

"Well, it's time for physical food. I'll be back. I do have to cook dinner, if we are both painting, then who will cook?"

"Mom, did you lose your mind or are you lost? You're Italian, and we are Italian because of that. We all know how to cook. Before I could talk, I knew how to cook. Can you please just help me finish the last of the painting here?"

I drift back to the Umbrian morning in my bed, and I glance at the walls in front of me. The discovery of the original fresco was completely by accident. I realize that if enough coats of paint are on an old plaster wall, the original painted plaster will reveal itself. It is a fact that new paint peels off of old plaster. At least the paint I used peeled off the white paint that the contractor had painted the walls. The actual process goes like this: a) I purchase paint; b) I paint; c) I realize the new paint is peeling off the wall, as well at the two coats underneath it. That was my first experience in Italian painting. With horror and disbelief, the only solution to correct the problem was to scrape off all the peeling paint. Using a spatula to scrape the paint—I had nothing else to use—began removing the two gallons of paint I had just applied to the wall. As I began scraping, the original fresco slowly revealed itself. This process was brutal, dusty, messy, and not at all easy. During this entire process, I thought, *What am I doing?* The next thought: *Rinny was right. The wall will speak to you and fill itself with the image it is meant to have.* I laugh to myself for a brief moment. The mural Rinny had painted was an abstract expression of her spirituality. While her room was cluttered with teenage debris, the fourteen-foot wall spoke of serenity, spirituality, and enlightenment. Each color in her design shimmered, reflecting the natural light during the day and the artificial light of the night. I realized that her symbolism was merely an abstract version of what lay before me.

Here before me, the spirit of the house has revealed the original intention for this wall. As I look around the room, I laugh to myself and reflect. Without even realizing it, here in my bedroom are statues of Buddha, St. Francis, Jesus, Virgin Mary, and Ganesh. My spiritual family is alive and well and now living in the Umbrian countryside with me. Enough of this brief memory—it is time for me to wake and rise from this pleasant slumber.

I surrender, and my foot again touches the cold terra cotta floor, this time followed by my other foot. The dreams of the night have given way to the aspirations of the day. That thought that wandered through my mind is still there, somewhere, and will continue to sleep just a bit longer before revealing itself to me.

I make the short journey to the *bayno*. The strange feature of it is its size, which I can only attribute to a miscommunication with the first contractor. What was to have been a portion of a bedroom was redesigned by the first contractor into one enormous bathroom. I feel as if I should have a fireplace or dining table added to fill in the enormous void. Sometimes it seems to me as if it takes ten minutes to walk from the shower to the toilet. The view from this bathroom is of the fields and distant villages. It truly is a welcome sight to anyone in the morning. The room is always filled by the breeze from the southern fields. I think back to Sarah and Pietro, my dear friends from Arezzo, who questioned me in dismay.

"Giovanna, this is such a large bathroom. What were you thinking and one so big without a bidet?" Sarah questioned.

"This is an Italian farmhouse," I explain, "not a French villa. Do I really need a bidet?"

"Italians like bidets," she said.

"But bidets are not Italian. Why do Italians want a bidet?" I asked.

"We like them. We are used to them. We are Italian, and you are only part Italian. Do you want an Italian bathroom?" she asked.

"I don't want an Italian bathroom if it means I need a French bidet."

I walk across the expanse of the bathroom and open the antique chestnut wardrobe that Pietro and Sarah gave to me. The wardrobe is enormous, at least eight feet high and five feet wide. It is basically what I consider a walk-in closet and certainly the only piece of furniture that fits the scale of the room. I look over my simple collection of clothes. It's all black. Everything matches, and there are two of everything—shirts, pants, sweaters, and dresses. Most Italians have closets that resemble a Prada or Armani store. Each item is in place, folded, stacked, and ready.

I, on the other hand, share my humble assortment of apparel with the linens, blankets, and towels for the entire house. It's easy and straightforward and fits my lifestyle here.

Clothing is important here. The colors and styles denote one's career. The *Carabinieri* and *polizia* have beautiful Armani suits that are always impeccable. I love watching them walk down the street. There is pride in their step, never rushing, glancing to the right and left as they make their daily rounds through town. The white leather holster and shoulder bag are accessories and necessities—a secure place for a pistol and a convenient and beautiful container for papers and documents. There are no bulging pockets stuffed with wrappers or money. They are a fashion statement unto themselves. The older men in Villastrada and most rural towns wear a hat, button-up sweater or vest, a standard brown or gray pair of slacks, and what we in America call a sports jacket. The clothing is always well kept, yet shows its long-lived life. The older women, in their black stockings, wear scarves tied only once under their chins, depending on the hour or chore, with or without an apron. Their dresses are all cut from the same pattern—in the country, this lifestyle is preserved. I finish dressing, close the wardrobe, and descend to the *cucina*. (kitchen). The wooden shutters are closed; the *casa* is still sleeping. The church bells ring. It is time to awaken from slumber. I open the shutters and doors, and the glory of the golden sun and a gentle warm breeze fills the room.

Morning here starts with coffee—the first cup of coffee is always at the local café. I walk to the small café in town. The rooster again assures me I'm on time—time, again that man-made condition. The wind is becoming stronger. The birds take to the branches, holding on for dear life, yet the sun is warm and welcome. I walk up the driveway through Gina and Mario's yard. It is a steep hill. It takes a few days to acclimate to walking here. Turning onto the main street, I approach the café. Small vehicles, scooters, and bicycles line the sides of the main road. I think to myself, *Cappuccino*. My body cannot wait, and my mouth begins to water in anticipation of the joy. My blood consists of coffee, water, and *vino*. Why would one drink anything else? The café is more of a wake-up for the body, while the coffee is specifically destined to wake the mind. The townspeople gather for their morning social. "Townspeople" refers specifically to the men of the town. Outside, the benches are filled with men, hands moving, and voices in an aria. Inside, the men never sit; they always stand, laugh, and talk of the news events posted outside on the front wall of the café. During the summer, a sheet of beads hangs in the doorway to protect the interior from unwanted flying pests.

On an outside sign board, large black letters tell of the day's top news stories. The posting of these three large posters is Gino's job—he's the older gentleman who started this café many years ago. He takes pride in this chore. Every morning he gently unfolds six posters, reading and reviewing each one carefully, to decide which will hold the place of honor. The placement position he follows is always first the major national news, followed by a major sports victory, and then the most pressing local event. Here, paper information is still the foothold of the news. This small rural café carries more international newspapers than most newsstands in major cities in the United States and certainly in more languages. Italians are a people who love to be informed, merely as a means to an end. Talking is one of their favorite pastimes, and it is not limited to any specific age or gender. The café sometimes sounds more like the Senate floor than a café. Opinions are extremely important. The need to be informed is not an option; it is the norm.

I begin to drift off, lost in the aria of voices. I order my cappuccino and decide to walk across the street to the vine-covered pergola that overlooks my farmhouse, fields, and olive grove, along with the distant views of the mountain and small villages that dot the horizon. The voices of the men outside the café carry across the street, and occasionally an outburst of disagreement breaks the soothing voices. The cappuccino is delicious. The neon green of the fields is overwhelming to my eyes, but my mind is completely at peace. The church bells begin tolling and bring me back. It is time to return to Olivetta. It is time to say *bon giorno* to the men outside the café. I know full well this will take more than a generic *bon giorno*. Greetings in this small town are a sign of respect and acknowledgement of one's achievements throughout life. I find it always best to address the older members of the town first. Certainly if Paulo is sitting outside, he will be first on my list.

Walking back to the farmhouse should take me approximately five minutes. In Italy, everything takes five minutes, but an Italian five minutes can take fourteen to thirty minutes. One might wonder about the disparity in time. Time is only relevant when needed. Italy has yet to find the "when needed." The main street is clean, polished, and full of life in the morning. The men and women of the town take to the street early—I mean, Italian early. No one gets up at the crack of dawn in Villastrada, except for the town's rooster. The famous rooster of Villastrada must be a dozen years old with only half his vocal cords. Every morning he calls out the awakening of day; hopeless, his song is half sung. The birds in the trees tease at him. This reminds me of *Peter and the Wolf*:

"What kind of bird are you if you can't fly?"

"What kind of bird are you if you can't swim?"

Only here the birds call out

"What kind of bird are you if you can't sing?" and the rooster replies,

"What kind of birds are you if you can't hear my song?"

The only other character to rival the song of the rooster is the deceitful village dog. Every day he takes his constitutional with his owner. Up and down the main street the two travel, the little dog always ten meters in front of the old gentleman. The gentleman carries his walking stick in his left hand, though he never appears to have any need for it.

The deceitful dog of Villastrada is as cute as a button, with more breeds in him as one can imagine. Quietly and submissively, he walks up to you, wagging his tail as if you are his owner or at least his best friend. He lies down in front of you and turns on his back, patiently waiting for you to bend down. Who wouldn't pet this cute little dog? Then, as you approach him, he anticipates your every move. He immediately growls, attempts to bite any piece of flesh that is within striking distance, and starts barking insanely. The barking sends everyone out of their homes. Outside of the initial flesh wound, you feel completely and totally like a fool. The owner calls the dog. The dog jumps at the command, wagging his tail, and returns to his rightful owner's side. Stunned and senseless, you regain control. This dog is a one-man police department for the entire town. Only visitors or strangers are fool enough to fall for the dog's trick more than once. An amazing part of this is that everyone who comes to visit Villastrada is warned, yet each believes he will be the one to break this predictable behavior.

I have made my way halfway up the street. The women are setting out their linens, rugs, and towels on the clotheslines that are connected from one balcony to the next. Their garments hang on a drying rack. Their bodies are perched over the wrought-iron railings, and the morning greetings begin. *Ciao, ciao.* Every *ciao* is expected to be followed by at least five minutes of how everyone fared last night. "*Come va?*" "How are you" is a trick phrase. Though *come va* means "how are you," it is perceived as "Tell me all your woes and ailments today." Everyone takes advantage of this confused translation and proceeds to explain the condition of life and health of each family member. Normally, my response is brief, and always followed by *e tu* ? (and you). I am granted a pass, as the women know my Italian is limited.

The women of Villastrada keep an eye out for me. If I am *solo* (alone), I can be sure that dinner and lunch invitations will follow. Having greeted the women immediately in my view, I decide to take the shortcut back though Mario and Gina's, thinking I can now make up for that lost time. But then, I remind myself there is no time here in the countryside. You can't make it up if you don't have it. I slow down and enjoy the dew on the grass beneath my feet. The sky is a brilliant blue with pure white clouds that fill the entire horizon. I have noticed that these heavenly beauties never seem to obstruct the sun; they always seem to linger just above the horizon. I stop and look at my neighbor's chicks, pigs, and rabbits. The birds are busy in the fields, looking for any seed or grain that might have been left behind. The hawk circles above the fields, waiting for the small mice to come into view. They glide in circles, working the air streams, saving their energy. Within a few moments, one dives down into the grass at the edge of the field. A victory for the hawk means a defeat for the field mouse. I know that soon, Rose and Stefano will begin the day's work in the olive grove. I had best be at the farmhouse to greet them when they arrive.

Chapter 10
Neighbors

I can hear the sound of the old car coming down the driveway. Rose and Stefano arrive in their green Fiat Panda, the typical Italian small countryside car. The car has lived three lives and shows its loyalty with small spots of rust and scratches. I get ready to work on the terrace area with the anticipation that Rose will have a predetermined task for me. As is traditional, we kiss and then tell each other the morning news. Then Stefano and Rose are off to work in the olive grove. Small fires are set in the olive grove. Smoke engulfs the fields, reminding me of the early morning fog. The smell of burning olive branches is a trademark of this region and season.

How do I explain Rose? Rose is not only an ant—meaning she can carry more than twice her weight—but she's also a wise sage. Yesterday I purchased some gardening supplies—a rake, hoe, and gloves—at the local hardware store. The rake appeared ridiculously small, but my thought was that Italians conserve on space and are small people like me, so this must be the official Italian rake. Now, Rose comes up from the grove and sees me struggling with the rake. She uses all of her strength not to fall over in laughter. She takes the rake from my hand. With three twists and two turns, what is a mini-rake turns into a fully extended rake; the biggest rake you could ever imagine. She explains the proper Italian use of the rake, and we move on. Italian rakes are engineering wonders; you can change the size, change the angle of the teeth, and change the length of the rake itself.

A pile of brush lying next to the house was making me crazy. I wanted to burn that pile just make it go away. But not understanding the rule about burning in Italy, I thought it best to wait for some advice from Rose. As if she is reading my mind, Rose informs me it is time to burn. *"Buciare, buciare."* The olive branches in the grove are burning. Why not burn the entire property? With that, she removes a match and a piece of flint from her pocket, and we are ready for an inferno—proof to Rose that we are Umbrian farmers.

Should I worry about the *machina*, the *casa*, and the neighbors? Obviously not, Rose is in charge and has been in charge for decades. The piles of dried shrubs ignite. I notice there is an additional supply of fuel for this fire. I walk up the small hill behind the *casa* and begin removing the foliage from last fall. Rose calls, "Giovanna."

Now, when Rose calls "Giovanna," Giovanna listens. Stopping dead in my tracks, I look over my shoulder. Rose produces a machete that Genghis Khan would be proud of. Up the hill, like an ant, she cuts away the spoils of last season. We will have an inferno, under her direction and guidance. I follow behind and pick up the felled fuel. The inferno is most impressive; every neighbor in every town surrounding this farm is aware we mean business. Much to my dismay, Rose has found additional fuel. Last year's corn crop is today's fuel.

"Giovanna."

I run; I pull, lug, and haul everything that has no sense of life left in it. The inferno will live. Rose smiles and places her hands on the side of her face. In Rose's eyes, Giovanna will be an Italian farmer after all. Rose is proud of herself and her student.

Our work is not done. A truck had driven onto the property

during the rainy month of February and created a crater matched only by the photos from the lunar landing. Rose and Giovanna will correct those injustices to the land and the beauty of the Italian countryside. Somewhere out of Rose's back pocket, a hoe is produced. Providing the required tool at the exact moment is her forte, something she and she alone has mastered. Rose sets off to work, moving the land. This is by no means an easy feat. The land has hardened from the lack of rain. The debris, bricks, and stones from the house restoration add to the difficulty of the task. The soil has become crushed concrete. Rose not only manages to remove the ruts but does so with little sign of a struggle. I am reduced to raking up rocks and debris from the restoration of the house. I believe all is going exceptionally well—inferno blazing, earth moving, rocks raked.

But Rose stops. "Giovanna."

"*Si*, Rose?"

Putting down her hoe, she proceeds to inform me how to put the rocks in the pail. I never thought about a proper way to place rocks in a pail. According to Rose, the proper way is simple and efficient. I was making it more difficult than necessary. The pail is to be turned on its side. The rocks are then scooped in. When the pail can hold nothing more, it is set upright and taken to the proper location for disposal. To merely toss rocks in a vertical pail is foolish and certainly not efficient. I laugh to myself. I have the knowledge I need for rock moving. Humble, yes I am humble, this woman works harder than anyone I've ever seen. She also has turned the art of working the land into a science. We continue our quest to return the land to its natural state.

Everything appears to have a place and an appearance that must be maintained. Living on the Tuscany/Umbria border enhances this reality. Every morning, the townspeople sweep the street and doorways in front of their homes. Windows sparkle; wooden doors, if varnished, glisten. Rose now advises me that the varnish on my doors and windows should be refinished. I hate varnishing, and I am certainly not good at it. The varnish on the doors and windows in Umbria is impeccable; certainly beyond my talents. I assure her I will take care of it in the near future. The ancient doors of the past are given respect. The faded paint tells its own story of over a hundred years. While some areas are as perfect as the day they were laid, others have loosened bearing the layer before them. This is more than a memory. The doors are clean and hardware is given permission to remain rusted and old. On the exterior walls, places where plaster is lost now expose the beauty of the mason's craft with pride. The revealed brick allows a story to unfold, unveiling a mystery as to who laid these bricks, who made them, and what tales they can tell. Ancient pride and glory are now exposed—a past life exposed. I think of Rose's front door. It's perfect. I must have my doors and windows refinished.

"Giovanna."

I look up. I am doing exactly what I have been told, in exactly the way I have been taught.

Rose says she has to return to Stefano to burn the additional olive branches. It is as if Stefano telepathically said, "Time to come back." Rose puts her hoe back in her mysterious pocket. Within three minutes, she is back with Stefano. The cut olive branches are ablaze. The wind's voice rustles the branches and leaves, directing the smoke to fill the fields to the south. The smoke takes on the shapes of the white clouds, filling the horizon. The land and sky become one. The smell of the burning branches acknowledges the movement of season and time.

In the fields, Rose works with Stefano. As the branches fall, she collects them like an ant on a mission to gather every grain of food left behind. Stefano and Rose are, in a way, one being—a symphony of life. Their joys and sorrows resonate. There is a collective conscience between them. When they work, there is a silence and yet a song of laughter as if each speaks silently. Stefano and Rose are a gift, but it is never to be forgotten that Rose is in charge. Stefano seldom contradicts her. Her commands are barked out and always carried out. For me, this is sometimes difficult. Later, I question why I so blindly listen, and I question where my voice is. I pay attention to the voice of the farmland, the wind making its presence known, passing through leaves and branches. The wind directs the smoke from the infernos away from the house.

I move rocks. The gratification of returning beauty to a place of splendor brings me peace. My mind this morning is focused on the plants I purchased. Herbs, vegetables, and new pots of boxwoods and lavender must be planted. This thought brings back my childhood days of gardening.

Growing up with Italians is like growing up in a pod of whales, where everyone takes care of everyone. If you have a square foot of dirt, someone comes over to teach you how to plant it. My mind begins to wander. The inferno has consumed all available fuel, and the smoke subsides. Where might I set the plants? Rose will take care of them when I am not here. I look at the piece of land we are working and decide on a perfect garden spot. My thoughts turn back to my Uncle Nick.

Uncle Nick's house was on the main land, Long Island, New York. He would plant and pot anything and everything on his small parcel of land. Proud of his yield, when he arrived at my parents' house, a trail of tomatoes, peppers, squash, and herbs always arrived with him. He always wore a vest, fedora, small string tie, classic gray or brown Italian country-style pants, and suspenders. He always had two packs of spearmint gum in his vest pocket. The five-minute greeting was typical Italian: kisses and pinching of the cheeks. Then, we would be rewarded with a stick of gum. Uncle Nick would walk into the kitchen, take the bottle of rye off the cabinet shelf, fill a cup with coffee, and top it off with rye. After his morning constitutional, it was time to set out for work. He would empty his pocket of packets of seeds. His day's work lay on the table, but it was first things first with Nick. The first thing was making lunch for us. This was a labor of love and talent. There was pasta to make and meat to prepare. When Uncle Nick cooked, it was like an explosion in

151

the kitchen. No one ever noticed the mess until it was time for the children to clean up. I wondered how pasta sauce could end up on every surface and how every pot had a function in the preparation of this meal. It was a mystery to me.

After the kitchen duties were finished, Nick would go to the garden. He always took one of us with him to the garden. My brother seemed to be responsible for the peppers, Nick for the tomatoes—tomatoes were too important to leave with an inexperienced child—and I for whatever was left. The next project for Uncle Nick was the culling of the "farm animals," though they were not really "farm animals" but our pets. Chickens, rabbits, and geese would become dinner for Uncle Nick that night. I say this with love and respect. It took a long time to realize that while he was planting the garden and setting arbors for the grapes, he also helped himself to a pet rabbit or chicken here and there. When we were young, we were told, "Oh, one of your pet rabbits (or chickens) escaped. We can't seem to find it." The easy acceptance of chickens, geese, and rabbits escaping was a gentle gift from our parents. We did not realize the animals were the food factory for many family members.

While reflecting on my land and what Uncle Nick might envision for the garden space, I heard a voice call out, "Giovanna."

God, I love this woman, but she can drive me crazy. Somehow, she climbs in my mind and knows what question is rumbling around—and she will answer this rambling question.

Before I can call back, Rose calls again. "Giovanna." I'm in trouble now. She has called out "Giovanna" twice. In Rose's mind, she should only have to call a name once. She expects an immediate response. A second call means, in her mind, that I'm not paying attention. It drives her crazy. It drives me insane.

"Yes," I reply.

"The plants."

I know she is out of sight and break into complete laughter. "Yes."

"Where are you planting them?"

I immediately respond with the only answer God or good sense provides. "I don't know. You tell me." I think, *I love this woman. She is the soul of this land, and she alone can transfer part of her knowledge to me.* Without Uncle Nick here to help, Rose is my new guide.

Rose is now in sight. "The plants—where are you going to plant the plants?"

"I don't know, Rose. Can you help?"

Rose immediately informs me that the repotting I had worked on yesterday was *perfecto*. She again reminds me that I need to work on a "planting plan." Now, she presents me with the perfect "Rose planting plan," I know if there is any hesitation on my part, she will once again advise me. I have no intention of going down that road. I will do what the land and Rose tell me to do. I am a humble servant to years of experience and knowledge.

Rose reminds me that I left one basil plant outside last night. In the mind of Rose and God, this should never happen. The nights are still far too cold for a small basil plant. I should always remember to bring them inside during the night. Lesson learned; I assure Rose it will never happen again.

"I am sorry, Santa Maria."

Why this woman should be my saint and guide me with patience, I am only sure Uncle Nick has something to do with it. I believe he visits Rose in her dreams and asks her to provide guidance where he left off about twenty-six years ago, when it was time for him to move to the next garden—heaven.

Right now, my conversation with Rose intensifies. This means that when I get lost in translation and say, "*Non capisco*" (I don't understand), Rose hears, "Talk louder; it will increase my ability to understand." In fact, the only thing it does is increase my risk of losing my hearing. I think I should have listened closer at my father's family dinner table and learned Italian, as well as learned how to create a garden and an inferno. At the same time, I think of the packet of sunflower seeds I purchased at the hardware store. Was I a fool to think I could make this purchase without Rose finding out? I would have to plant them, they would grow, and the first question Rose would ask would be, "Why did you plant the sunflowers there?"

I believe this will be a late-summer surprise. Maybe she will believe that they were seeds from the last sunflower crop like the corn that pops up out of "nowhere." I assure myself we'll work it out. Stefano calls silently in Rose's mind. Rose looks at me and silently says she will be back. Before Rose leaves to help Stefano in the fields, she says *legna*, (firewood) remember the firewood, haplessly dumped in the middle of the driveway. The firewood needs to be moved and stacked. The tractor needs to pass to work the fields.

"The tractor cannot pass," she says.

My translation of this: Before the sun sets and the cock cries thrice, that firewood blocking the driveway had best be stacked, by age, size, and type. No questions asked.

"*Si, legna*," I respond.

"*Bravo*, Giovanna, *bravo*."

I had passed yesterday's test. Wood was stacked perfectly.

The burning and cutting and burning and cutting again draws me back to the burning and cutting of childhood. My mother would burn the "bank" at our home on the island. "Burning the bank" literally meant lighting a geographic feature on fire, even though it was within forty yards of the island's entire oil supply. She lit a match, tossed it onto the dried shrubs and boom—she was burning the bank. Someone always forgot to ask if anyone had the garden hose. The town would later decide that it would be prudent to have a fire truck on hand in the unlikely event that the fire raged out of control.

Rose's fire would put the bank fire to shame. Our fire roars; the entire countryside is alight. Smoke from every farm sends signs of the turning of the season. I think back to the stereotypical image of American Indians, sending smoke signals, and think, *we have it. Toss those cell phones out. We have matches, olive branches, and shrubs. We can now talk.*

Rose and I have the entire farm ablaze. There does not appear to be any alarm among the neighbors or the fire department, though I'm not even sure if a "true" fire department exists here in the Umbrian countryside. I have seen a large building on the way to Perugia that claims it is a firehouse. It has a bell in a steeple, presumably for notifying firemen of a blaze. The large doors are always closed. It resembles something from a 1950s movie set. I did have one fire truck sighting. It was on the way to Chiusi—one fire truck and two firemen. They were performing roadside vehicle checks, a job normally reserved for the Carabinieri.

The church bells chime, and I realize I am to pick my federal marshal up at the Chiusi train station. I apologize and tell Rose I must pick up my friend, and we are going for lunch in town. Rose and Stefano invite my friend and me to their *casa* for lunch. My being a vegetarian makes it difficult for her to cook for me. It's not that I am a difficult eater. Basically, I will eat anything that is put in front of me, as long as it does not walk. I believe the difficulty for Rose is simply that she thinks I am not eating enough. Possibly, I will wither and blow away in the next strong wind. If such a fate were to occur, Rose certainly would not allow it on her watch.

I love being with them for lunch—it's Italian eating at its best. But today I politely decline. I run to the house to gather the keys for the car and my cell phone and then run to the car. The day is spectacular, the drive always a pleasure. On the way to Chiusi, I think about the two times I actually walked to the train station. Having done it once, there certainly was no need to attempt it a second time. But what is the saying? If you don't remember, you will relive. I learned my lesson—the only way to Chiusi for me now is in my little Fiat. I travel through the narrow streets of upper Chiusi and then make my descent down to lower Chiusi and head for the station. The parking lot is not full, which is a miracle; finding parking here is always a hurdle. I park the car, check the time, and then make sure I set the paper dial on the windshield—the dial allows the *poliza* to know when you arrived and when you have overstayed your allotted thirty minutes. I walk toward the station, through the open doors, and look up at the arrival sign. The train is delayed for one hour. This means I must go back and move the car to one of the parking areas that allow for four hours.

The walk back to the station this time is twice as far, but I have an hour to play before Mike arrives. I cross the street and decide to have an espresso outside at the café. People-watching in Italy is a valid occupation. Actually, as you get older, I believe it is a requirement. I enter the spotless café—the floors are clean enough to eat off them. The woman behind the counter takes my order and tells me she will bring it outside. I pick up a local paper and find an empty table. In the back of my mind, I'm a little nervous about the tardiness of the train. Usually a late train is reported as twenty minutes, which translates into the train's arriving within the hour. When the train is listed as one hour late that means it might not show up. If it does, it definitely will be more than an hour tardy. But I'm in Italy, and I realize I am a little jet lagged, so this is just what the doctor ordered. Then I have a brilliant idea. I can call Mike on his cell phone and find out what town he has just left. I dig through my bag, find my phone, and call his number. The phone rings and rings, but no one answers. He must be in one of the twenty tunnels between here and Roma. I can smell the coffee, and then my waitress arrives with the dark, robust coffee and two small cookies on the side of the saucer. I look across at the train station and the line of little white taxis waiting for a passenger. All the taxi drivers are gathered in a circle, talking to each other—hands waving, bursts of laughter, slaps on the back. The life of the male taxi driver is so very easy. They all wear vests and their signature hats. A group of travelers begins to empty out of the station's opened doors. Most just carry briefcases or pocketbooks. After the crowd dissipates, a middle-aged couple carrying six bags appears. They are definitely American, They wear their matching outfits—middle age, middle America, in the middle of a small Italian town. The circle of cab drivers looks over at them and continues their conversation. The woman is in the lead and the husband attempts to navigate the luggage to the first cab in line. The woman goes over to the taxi; the men still are talking. I can imagine the conversation being something like this:

"How many taxis will it take to fit their entire luggage?"

"Three."

On cue, two drivers leave the circle and walk over to help the struggling husband. I can't image the couple's vacation is going very well. The taxi drivers load the luggage, and the woman takes the lead taxi, while the man squeezes into the second. Another duplicate couple appears. The event is repeated. The line of taxis is now reduced to two cars, and their drivers laugh and shake their heads, I decide to give Mike another call and see where he might be. Again, there is no answer. I begin to wonder if he missed the train or if maybe he had to fly back to the States and didn't have a chance to call. I check my missed calls, but there was none. I finish my coffee and settle my bill. I check the status of the train. The arrival board still has the train as one hour late. I decide to busy myself and go to the bank. Then I realize it is siesta. There are no banks open, no shops, and no post office. Basically, the café, the train station, and a small restaurant are my only options. I don't want to eat, thinking Mike will be starving when he arrives. I decide on a glass of wine and some cheese at the restaurant down the street. The restaurant has outside dining and is on a quiet street, a perfect place to idle away time.

The air is warm, and the gentle breeze wraps itself around me. *Thank you, St. Francis, Buddha, and God for this beautiful gift of Italy.* My heart races, I take a deep breath and remember all that were here before me and all the lives that made this wonderful country.

The masons' and artists' work still lives on today. *Grazie.* I walk into the restaurant, and a woman greets me. I tell her I would just like some cheese and a glass of the house wine, and ask if I could sit outside.

"Certainly, I will bring it out to you."

I return outside and sit down. I realize that I need some things at the house, and this is a perfect time to write a list. It's just like having an Italian plan. I forgot Sarah might be coming down from Arezzo, either tonight or tomorrow. I'd best call her. Again, I search for my phone. My reputation is that I lose everything—phones, keys, glasses, debit cards, anything small enough to be misplaced. I find the phone this time in a jacket pocket and proceed to call Sarah. The phone rings. I hear *"Pronto,"* the voice of my Italian sister.

"Pronto, sono Giovanna."

"When did you arrive?" Sarah asks, "And how long are you staying? You never stay long enough?"

"Yesterday, and not long enough, but I hope you are coming to see me tonight for a sleep-over or tomorrow for the day. Is that possible?"

"I don't have anyone to cover the store, so I can't come tonight. I'll come tomorrow, and we can spend the day together. I'll stay the night, because in Italy, shops don't open on Sunday or Monday morning. They open on Monday afternoon."

"This is another reason I love it here. I'm waiting in Chiusi for this federal marshal I met on the plane yesterday," I calmly state.

"What federal marshal? What is he doing, coming to Olivetta, and what about Robert?" she sternly demands.

"First, he's a federal marshal, and I invited him up. He was to be on the 11:40 train from Termini, but it is late. I invited him to the country because I thought it would be good for him to get out and see how the local Italians live. He's not a murderer; he really is a nice guy," I finished, hoping to instill some calm.

"Yeah, nice guy. Did you see his badge? Did you see if he had a gun? What's his last name? I bet you don't know it, right?" Sarah was in her protective mode, and she wanted answers.

"He's fine. Maybe his friends are saying the same thing. Who is this woman? And maybe she will kill you and bury you on her farm," I laughingly say.

"Okay, I get it. So he's a nice guy; works for the federal government, call me when he arrives and let me know how everything goes. You forgot to call me and tell me you were here. So, promise me you will call."

"I will, I will. I promise you that and more. How is everyone? Can Zara come and play with us? Oh, I'm here for I don't know how long but hopefully two weeks. Robert is going to come over to learn how to prune those olive trees. Actually, I want both of us to know how to prune those olive trees."

Sarah understands I'm trying to be a good Italian farmer. It takes time, energy, and most of all, patience to observe those who have worked this farm for so many years.

"*Ciao e baci.*" I will see you tomorrow" Sarah replies.

"*Ciao e baci.*"

I put the phone back in my bag and look at the pen and notepad. It is time to make my list for the market. The café is full—all of the outside tables are now taken by travelers, many of whom are waiting for the train from Roma to go to Florence. My waitress appears with a small cheese plate and my wine. I look at the cheese—a young talegio, pecorino, and Fontana; a perfect combination and enough to hold me over until Mike arrives. My phone rings.

"*Pronto.*"

"*Pronto, sono Roberto.*"

"Robert, what are you doing up so early in the morning?" I am baffled.

159

"What you and your federal marshal are doing is more important," he laughs.

"I am alone in Chiusi. The train from Roma is late, and I decided to have some cheese and wine at the little restaurant down the street. Did you and the girls have a good dinner last night?" Then Robert inquires.

"So, you are sitting at the restaurant down the street from the station? When Mike arrives give me a call. I love you, *ciao e baci.*"

The message was calm but concerned.

Now back to my cheese, wine, and my list of to-gets. *But why did Robert call so early? He really can't be worried. Did Zoe and Gabrielle put him up to calling to make sure I was alive and not tied to the dining room table? Silly—they know me better than that. I am the crazy lady, but I am not insane.* It is now time to enjoy my cheese and wine and the warmth of the day.

"*Giovanna!*" a voice calls out. It is familiar, but it can't be the voice I am hearing. "*Giovanna, come sta?*" I know that voice. I just hung up with that voice on the phone. It's Robert. I look up, and standing in front of me is the man I love, the man who just called me. "I was at the station and thought I'd give you a call."

"Robert. What are you doing here? I thought you were coming in two days to work with Stefano, pruning the trees. You're here! I just talked to you last night and to Gabrielle and Zoe—you were all to have dinner together. I'm confused." It was a plea.

Robert leans over and kisses me—a kiss that stops my heart, and I beg for another. He holds me in his arms, and I know I am loved, and this man will forever stand with me.

"My dear—a term you hate, but my dear—the girls and I decided that it was crazy for me to not be here with you, especially at this time. They love you so much. They said they would drive me to the airport. They have each other and wanted me to be with you. I have to admit, I agreed with them. I'm here. I'm with you. I love you." Tears rolled down his checks, and a smile came over his face.

"I love you so much. I love my children so much. I love Italy so much." I smiled and wept.

"Can I sit down?"

"No, only after another kiss."

I felt as if I was in a Fellini movie—the man I love calls and within three minutes is sitting before me. Robert understands the beauty and love that people here have to offer and freely give to everyone. I look over at him and see the gentle, kind, giving man he is.

The waitress returns and asks for Robert's order.

Robert looks at me and asks, "How is the cheese?"

"It is delicious," I answer. "You should have a mix of cheese and meats. You must be starving by now." Robert nods, and I order his snack. I can't believe he is here. It's a miracle. "Tell me how you got here. You must have flown to Florence, because *Tranitalia* is late from Roma."

"Simple: left JFK and went to your favorite Swiss city, Zurich, then flew from Zurich to Florence and train to Chiusi. All flights were on time. The train was on time. I actually arrived ten minutes early in Chiusi. Maybe it's because the Roma trains are *retardo* that my train arrived early. The flight was unremarkable—two movies and sleep. The plane was only half full—plenty of room to stretch out. I did have a little snack from the bicycle food car, on the train." He smiled his gentle smile and held my hand.

"Did you meet a federal marshal or anyone interesting?" I ask.

Robert looks over at me. There is something he is not telling me.

"What do you have to tell me?" I ask. "What is going on? I know you, and I know that when your lips do that funny thing, something is up. What's up?"

"Well, there are a couple of things," he admits. "First, I

sent my résumé to an Irish telecom company, and they want to interview me."

"You have got to be kidding. Where will you be located?"

"The position is in Dublin. It's a great senior position. I can't believe it. The man I am to interview with is traveling for a week. When he gets back, we will video conference. I thought I could use Sarah's computer to Skype. I really can't believe it. I have sent so many résumés out and nothing seems to happen. Then, out of this random job opening, I get an interview." He is beaming and laughing.

"We might move to Dublin? Maybe I can finish up my master's at the university there. That would keep me busy. I presume I can come with you." I realize that this is a big assumption on my part. We are together, but that does not mean I am automatically invited.

He sees the desperate look on my face and immediately responds. "Wherever I go, you had better be with me. I wouldn't have it any other way. I love you." He speaks with passion.

I jump from my seat and embrace him. The warmth of the sun and the warmth of his love give me at peace. We both laugh irrepressibly.

"Now, the second thing I have to tell you," Robert continues, "is that the Zoe and Gabrielle gave me something for you. I'm glad Mike the Marshal is not here to hear this. You know the question that they ask as you go through airport security—'Did anyone give you anything?'"

I interrupt with laughter. "That's not what they mean. They mean strangers. Mike will actually find that very amusing. Oh, I should try to call him again to see where the train is. Hold on one second." I rummage for the phone, find his number, and call. The phone call goes directly to voicemail. "Robert, it's strange I can't get through to Mike. Do you think something might have happened or that he changed his mind?"

Robert looks at me and says, "Nothing has happened. He is either stuck on the train in a tunnel or realized that he had been invited to a crazy lady's country farmhouse and had second thoughts." He starts to laugh.

"You're right. Either seems possible, although I prefer the former option. Let's celebrate your interview and the possibility of a job, and your early arrival here in the Italian countryside, *Salute*."

We raise our glasses to salute our good fortune. It is still early, and Robert is still hungry. We decide to share pasta with mushrooms. Our waitress reappears and I place our order of pasta and ask for another bottle of water. We sit silently for a few minutes and enjoy the warmth of the afternoon. Two sparrows land on the table next to us, looking for an ort from the previous diners, but the table was devoid of any food. I take a piece of bread from the basket and place it on the table.

"You are going to be sorry you did that." Robert declares.

"Why will I be sorry?" I want to know.

"Those two are just scouts. They're out to see if we are willing to surrender our peace. I guarantee there is a flock of sparrows in the tree, and once they see our willingness to provide a banquet, they will descend upon us in unruly numbers."

"Stop—that is ridiculous."

Before I can utter another word, there are at least ten more sparrows looking at me. It is at this point that our waitress brings our water, and the pending threat of a flock of sparrows is erased.

"You were just saved." Robert points up to the tree where the flock had retreated.

Our pasta arrives, and I realize that it is getting late. The train with Mike should be arriving in ten minutes. We finish eating and gather our belongings. I reach in my bag and realize I had forgotten to pick up the money from the desk at the farmhouse.

"Do you have any euros on you?" I ask. "I used what I had in my pocket."

Robert shakes his head. "Giovanna, you forget so much

and remember so much more. How much is it anyway—two euros?"

"Well, it is actually quite pricey. The total is nine euros. I only dine at the best places," I say and burst into laughter.

We leave for the train station. The arrival board now has the train from Termini as canceled. The next train is expected to arrive in two hours, but it is reported as three hours late. *Looks like Tranitalia and Marshal Mike will not be arriving today.*

Robert asks, "What is the next plan for today? *Casa?*"

I can tell he is tired, but we need some supplies at the house. "*Casa dopo,* after we stop at the market. It won't take long. We can stop in Villastrada."

Robert falls asleep on the way home. I look over at him and realize he is completely exhausted. I turn on the radio and enjoy the music. We arrive in town. The market is open, but I remember I've left my money at the house, so I will have to return. I turn down the dirt driveway. The car bounces over the ruts, and Robert startles.

"We're here already?" he asked. "I thought we had to stop at the market for supplies."

I laugh. "I left my money at the house. No supplies without money."

As we pulled up to the house, Rose is approaching the olive grove. She looks over at the car, stops in her tracks, and heads our way.

"She wants to know who my friend is. I told her I was unable to have lunch with them today because I was meeting a friend at the station."

Robert looks at me and then at Rose. "Giovanna, you are in trouble. She will want to know why I'm in the car. Then she will inquire as to why you told her I would be here in two days, and I'm here today. You will have to explain the train, the phone, and the fact you don't have a plan and did not pick up the items from the market. You know this is going to take the better part of an hour to satisfy her curiosity." He looks over at me and just beams a smile that understands everything.

Robert rolls down his window and call out "*Ciao* Rose."

"Roberto?" she calls out with a pronounced annoyance. Rose wants to know where my friend is, and so on. Robert called it down to the last detail. After a thorough interrogation, she finally is satisfied and walks back down the hill to the olive grove. I had asked forgiveness for not helping this afternoon and promised that both Roberto and I would be ready, willing, and able in the morning.

Robert looks over at me. "Do we really have to work now?" he asks, almost as if pleading for his life.

"No, I told her we would work in the morning and that we were grateful for her help."

"Thank God," he mutters.

We head for the house. I realize that Robert needs sleep, so I decide to go to the market on my own. "It's up to bed for you. I'll go the market. Do you need anything?"

He shakes his head and gives me a kiss on the forehead. "Wait. Join me, please."

I can't resist. I am tired. We can go to the market later.

Upstairs, we climb into bed, curl up in each other arms, and within a minute are both fast asleep.

Chapter 11
Gift

A voice awakes us. "Giovanna, Giovanna, Roberto, Roberto."

It must be Rose, and I must be in trouble for something. Robert opens his eyes and smiles, knowing full well Rose has something she wants us to attend to immediately. I climb out of bed. My thoughts are still in the dream I was startled from. I call out, "Si, Rose."

I walk downstairs, and Rose is standing just outside the open door. She directs me outside and points to the car. I can't image what might be wrong with the car. It looks fine. I think maybe she and Stefano want a ride home, but no. Rose thinks that I did not park in the right spot. I can't understand how I could have parked in the wrong spot. It's my driveway and my car, and it looks just fine to me.

She points to the spot where I should park and shakes her finger at me. "You must park there, not there," she commands.

I'm too exhausted to argue. I follow her commands and immediately walk over to the car and park it in the Rose-designated spot. As I begin to walk back, I see her smile the Rose smile, the Rose-is-in-charge smile, but Rose is not finished. She points to the open side door of the house.

Rose says, "Giovanna, the door should never be open. You

167

should close the door. Animals might get in. Always close the door."

Another commandment directed from Rose. Moses only had ten; Rose's commandment list just keeps growing. I apologize and promise I will close the door, though I know this is a commandment I cannot possibly keep. I look over Rose's shoulder and see Robert descending the stairs.

He calls out, "Rose, how are you?"

This is a curse and a blessing. Robert does not speak enough Italian to hold a conversation with Rose. This means he has trapped me. Rose will now repeat everything she has just commanded, and I must interpret it for Robert. It is a way to display her dominance. I glare at Robert. It is only the ringing of my cell phone that saves me from this lecture.

"*Pronto*," I answer the cell phone.

"*Pronto, mia sorella.*" I hear Sarah's voice on the other end of the phone.

"*Ciao*, are you coming down and when?" I am so excited.

"I'm not sure when, but I will give you a call and let you know. Marshal Mike around?" she giggles.

"No, not Marshal Mike, but Robert made a surprised arrival."

"Can I talk to him?"

I go outside where Rose still has Robert trapped. I have to hold back my laughter. Rose is not quite ready to give up the floor.

"Robert, it is Sarah. She wants to talk with you."

Upon hearing Sarah is on the phone, Rose looks at me and demands to speak with her. I am now thinking, *Oh my God, poor Sarah. Our phones will run out of minutes before Rose finishes.* I unwillingly surrender the phone into Rose's hand, but I know there is no alternative. Rose's words become more rapid and build to a crescendo. I look at Robert and shake my head. Rose finally stops talking, hands the phone to Robert, and says *ciao.* Robert takes the phone into the house. I stand alone in the middle of the driveway, wondering, *How did this happen?*

Robert's laughter echoes through the open windows and doors and the stone house. I walk up to my favorite outdoor haven and sit down. I look down the driveway and see Rose on her march home. The clouds cast their shadows across the field. It reminds me of the leaves on the stucco wall yesterday at lunch by the lake. Dancing a ballet here, the canvas is much larger and the dance much more languid. I raise my hands to my eyes and lower my head. It is time for a moment of meditation. There is complete silence.

"Giovanna. Giovanna."

I automatically recoil.

"Giovanna." The voice is Robert's, from inside the house.

"*Si.*"

"Where are you hiding?"

I smile; he will find me. My response is silence. I look down from my perch. He is walking down the driveway. I laugh, and he turns around.

"I'm hiding from Rose," I say with a laugh.

"Wow, I had forgotten how intense she can be. She wore Sarah out. By the way, Sarah wants us to go to Arezzo for lunch tomorrow. Then we can all come down together for a sleepover."

"Let's walk up to the market and get some supplies and discuss our options. I'll get my bag."

Robert calls after me, "Can we take the car, please? I'm a little tired, and we—"

"That's fine. I'll get the keys," I reply.

I walk out to the car, and Robert is in the driver's seat. I think to myself, *He's not tired; he just loves driving in Italy.* I hand over the keys, and we bounce down the rugged dirt driveway. For some reason, when Robert traverses the driveway, he bottoms out approximately five times each way.

I look and smile at him and say, "You always do that—the

bottoming out with the car. I think you just like the sound of the car rubbing against the earth."

He laughs and says.

"Remember, Tom said when you return the car they never look underneath, just around all four sides." I roll my eyes and say.

"Both you and Tom are totally crazy."

We pass my neighbor's house, the old gentleman who sits outside on his patio, next to his garden. He has his fedora on and his vest, and his little black cat complacently sits on his lap. We stop, roll the window down, and greet him. His face fills with a smile, and he slowly raises his hand, producing a gentle wave.

We pull onto the main road and look for a place to park in front of the market. All spots are taken, and all the parking at the post office across the street is full. It is market time in Italy. Robert turns around. We head for the café.

"It actually would have been closer if we had walked from the house." My comment goes unnoticed.

"If we'd parked at the house, I couldn't drive, and I love to drive in Italy," Robert says. I shake my head and acknowledge this statement of truth. We pass the café, filled with life. There are people outside, sitting on benches. The pergola is set for tonight's pizza dinner. Robert turns the car around at the cemetery, and we head back to the market. He finds a place in front of the beautiful brick church, Santa Maria del Grazie. Robert jumps out and runs to my side of the car.

"*Senora*," he says as he opens the door for me.

"Trying to impress the Italian men with your culture?" I ask.

"We Irish need as much help as we can get. I don't want to look disrespectful to you, *senora*."

I realize I really do love him. "*Prego.*" My voice is soft and filled with grace.

He takes my hand and we head off to the market.

"You do have one thing going for you as an Irelander," I tell him. "Your mom gave you the right name. Just an addition of one vowel and your name is Roberto. I, on the other hand, have a total transformation. Joann—they don't even have a J in the Italian alphabet. It kind of makes me feel like a second-class citizen. Now that I think about it, how did my dad let my mom do that to me?"

"Are we talking about your mom? She could get your dad to do anything with her English determination." He barely finishes the statement before bursting into laughter. I give him my evil eye and shake my head. We arrive at the market. The automatic doors are open, allowing the spring breeze to enter this little miracle market. I look over and see Roberto, one of the owners. He is wearing his professional outfit, looking more like a doctor than the proprietor of a market. His long white coat, slightly open, tells everyone he works at the market. He comes over and kisses me and then gives me a warm embrace. My heart swells; my soul soars. "*Ciao, ciao.*" He smiles at Robert and then kisses and embraces him.

Robert is approximately a foot taller than Roberto. He bends down ever so slightly to make the embrace and then looks over at me and says, "I love Italy. I love Italy. There is nothing more beautiful, spiritual, or complete than this country and this beautiful country town."

I nod.

Roberto calls to his father and the greeting is repeated. Roberto then asks, "How long will you stay this time?"

"Forever, if possible," I respond.

We hug each other again. The aromas from a roasting pig fill the air. I love it, even though I'm a vegetarian. There is something intoxicating about that smell. Robert looks at me, and I know he will head directly to the meat counter to see how long before His loved *porchetta* will be ready. I head directly to the cheese counter. Roberto's brother is in charge of the cheese. When he sees me, he comes over, and we embrace. "*Pecorino, Parmesan e Gorgonzola, si?"* He knows what I love and proceeds to slice a piece of each for testing.

I raise my finger to the side of my face, *buono.*

"Pane?"

He smiles. *"Si."*

I head off to where I know I will find Robert. After the meat counter, the next most important item is the jet-fuel fire starter. I find him exactly where he should be. He is looking over the various options for fire starter.

"The green one," I simply state.

"Why the green one?"

"Because that is the one Rose uses. If she finds any other brand in the house, I get in trouble. I don't want a lecture from Rose on what jet-fuel fire starter I should use. Remember, I blamed you last time for leaving the door open and the lights on. So if you want to get a little of Rose's ire, go ahead and pick up the black box. I won't be held accountable."

"Whoa, there," Robert says. "If we take it out of the box, she won't know what color the box was, right?"

"Rose always knows. It's your scolding. I don't like playing with fire. I wouldn't go there if I were you."

"I'll tell her you did it."

"You can't. You're Irish, and the guilt would kill you. You will have to go to confession, say your penance, and still you will feel guilty for a week. It will cost me about five euros to light candles in the church to save your soul from guilt. So, pick up the green box, and let's get home before we miss the twilight. By the way, you are crazy too." I just shake my head.

Robert takes the green box and off we go to check out. We walk back to the car and load our supplies in the back.

I ask, "Do you want to go into the church and say a prayer and light a candle?"

"Sounds perfect."

The doors of the church are enormous with small people-size doors cut into them. The church is always open and has the scent of incense, flowers, and warmth. It again reminds me of being a small child. The holy water rests in an enormous marble carved fountain. We kneel and silently pray. I am grateful. I get up and go to the bank of candles. I realize the candles are part of the aroma of the church. I place my offering in the little tin slot and hear the euro drop to the bottom. I pick up a candle and use one of the illuminated ones to light mine. The gift of peace and humility fills me. One prayer lights the light of another. I bow my head and pray. I pray for everyone who used to sit around Uncle Nick and Aunt Lena's table and for all those who were never afforded that opportunity. The fading sunlight pierces the round window, illuminating the fresco at the side of the altar. *Thank all of you.*

Robert stands behind me.

"I think I covered everyone," I say.

He kisses me on my forehead. "You always think of everyone." he says, and he gently takes my hand. We bow and walk down the aisle. He opens the door. We are greeted by the voices of the town. He opens the car door for me; we are off. The journey home takes less than a minute but is filled with the sound of the bottom of the car scraping the earth. I look at him and shake my head,

"Well my love we are home. I will tend to the cheese, meat, bread and wine, and you can tend to the fire."

"Bravo, Robert, I'm in the kitchen, you are at the hearth."

I'm off to my domestic duties. Within five minutes, the fire is blazing, and I have plated the food and brought the wine and glasses to our little haven. Robert joins me.

"The honor of opening the bottle is yours as always, my love," I tell him.

Robert opens the bottle and pours two juice glasses of wine. Though we have wine glasses, it is sacrilegious for me to use them. Italians use juice glasses. The wine glasses are reserved for my American friends who can't wrap their minds around drinking wine out of a juice glass.

I raise my glass to make a toast. "To Lena, Nick, Mario, and Gina, by the grace of God, we are here today." I gaze out at the clouds as they dance across the sky, and their shadows are cast on the fields.

Robert turns on the Three Tenors, and the sounds echo through the thick stone walls and out through the open windows and doors.

"Have you seen the owl yet?" Robert inquires.

"No. I was not driving last night. He or she seems to love the signpost on the way into Castiglione del Lago. I did, however, hear the call late last night. These swallows and sparrows are making quite a bit of noise. I wonder if they are singing to the Three Tenors."

Robert responds, "They are just telling each other where they are and what branch they're on. It's a territorial thing. You have to get up to speed. They're not just birds. They all have names. Sure, the rooster is a pain in the ass, but he is a single-vocal-cord rooster who has dementia and just crows because he doesn't remember he has already crowed ten times. Actually, he is doing his job, or he would be in the roasting pan. I saw quite a few little chicks running around today. Tomorrow, I'll work with Stefano in the grove. I need to learn as much as possible about the trees and how they need to be tended. I might need you for some translation. Stefano is hard for even Sarah to understand."

"If you need me to translate, just whistle. I can pretend I understand Stefano, but it is more of a sign language combined with dialect Italian. If you are confident, you will understand. Just remember you are a foot taller than he is. Don't go into the trees until he tells you. You might be reduced to gathering branches. If you watch him, you will understand. The general concept is to trim from the center. I don't understand why, and no one has explained it to me. It's like the older men in town, playing cards. No one knows what the game is called, or at least they don't divulge the information. They certainly are not going to give the crazy American/Irish anything from the secret Italian male society." I break into laughter.

"You seem to have been embraced by them, though I'm sure the women look at you and wonder. They see you as a crazy Italian American who purchased a farmhouse without anyone's help. You travel back and forth alone. You have the house restored by yourself—to them, you don't make sense, crazy or not, but somehow or other they do love and care for you. It's like you are the orphan woman of Villastrada. Someone is always willing to watch after you. I know you said you had plans with Sonya tonight for pizza, but can we just stay here?" he pleads.

"That might be tough. Breaking a plan here is not that easy. However, when she comes to the house I will explain that you surprised me and are just a wee bit tired. We can have some snacks and wine here. I will promise to take her to Santa Maria Restaurant tomorrow night. That will be perfect." I have a plan. *Bravo.*

In fact, Pietro and Sarah are my saviors.

"Hey, where is Marshal Mike?" Robert asks. "You haven't heard a word from him. Should you give him another call?"

"You're right. I'll call now and see if I can reach him." I fumble to find the phone.

Robert looks at me and shakes his head. "You are so funny. You lose everything. What's really crazy is that every door in your house has its own key, and the last time I counted there were seven doors. Do you know where the keys are? I think you put the phone in your bag. By the way, your bag is downstairs in the entry, hanging on the hook. Do you want me to get it for you?"

"I would love that."

In a moment, he calls, "Giovanna. Giovanna."

Please tell me the phone is in my bag. His voice now reminds me of Rose when I failed to do what I was told to do.

"Giovanna."

"*Si.*"

"I can't find your bag or your phone. Any idea where it might be? Did you look in the pocket of your jacket? Can you look under the bed? When did you have it last? Should I look in the car?"

I know he is shaking his head and wondering how a woman can do so many things and still be so disorganized. I hear his voice again.

"I found it. You know where it was? It was in the bathroom."

He always seems to find it in the most inappropriate spot. I remain silent.

"Where is the charger?" he asks.

I have absolutely no idea where the charger is. Maybe it is in an outlet somewhere. After thinking a moment, I reply, "The charger must be in the desk. I don't take it to America because it doesn't work there."

"Giovanna, I love you, but you make me crazy. You should place the phone and the charger in one place when you come back to the house. That way, you will know where it is, though I truly believe you really don't care, because you always end up finding it. I'll bring the charger and phone up, and guess what? Put them together."

What can I say? Silence is my response.

Robert comes back upstairs, leans over, and kisses me. "This is why I love you, and this is why you love Italy—because in the end, it doesn't matter. You can be you—a Zen, Buddhist, Catholic crazy woman, and everyone still loves and cares for you."

His words resonate in my mind. What have we lost? What is missing from our life that makes this my haven? I stumble through the thoughts, lost and confused. The complications of living in the northeast of America, a hub of insanity fed by itself for itself, seems trite and, more important, unsustainable. The shield of humanity is lost to gala benefit for self-importance and vanities beyond comprehension. I sink momentarily into a pit of despair, silently vowing to never leave this moment of soul-searching truth. The truth, simplicity, lost to those without souls, humanity truly now extinct. A deepening moment of regret comes over me. Reality does rear her ugly head for all who choose to look.

"Giovanna? Giovanna, are you okay?"

I shake my head, solemn and speechless. My mind races through the labyrinth of time. Haven or heaven seem to be just ideological words of lost scholars. Truth—the demon that we constantly avert. Yet truth sits on our shoulders, daring us to tempt ourselves and the world. Joy is a luxury afforded to the wealthy, at least in their material minds. Joy for humanity is the pleasure derived from the simplicity of life.

"Giovanna."

This time I realize that my thoughts are too overpowering. "*Si.*"

"Giovanna, what are you thinking about?"

"What everyone never wants to think about, if that makes sense?"

My words seem dry and lifeless. Robert's face has a look of confusion. I realize I have been holding a pity party for humanity—those lost to life running on a treadmill in front of a television with their life connected to nothing. The talking heads on the television are lost to the music pumped into their being by technology, tethered to their lifelessness by a wire connected to their ears. They run nowhere except to escape their lifeless lives.

"Giovanna." His voice sounds urgent.

I look over and respond, "Just having a pity party for the soulless."

"Can I ask the party guests to leave? Sounds like a lifeless group."

"You're right; they are a lifeless group, which is why we are here, and it's time for that party to end. Sorry. I sank to the depths of despair for a moment, but it actually reminds me of how grateful for life one should be, and to always be gracious, and most of all carry kindness and love as a shield against the enemy of humanity. I was just traveling down the canyon of lost souls. For a moment, I forgot where I was and who I was with. Where were we, before my faithless journey began?"

Beethoven is now playing and life begins to fill my soul once again. The music fills my soul, and I remember the joy of life.

"Are you really okay?" Robert asks. "I know this is an extremely hard time for you. Are you all right?" I hear urgency and a profound sense of love in his voice.

"We all have a moment that takes us down a path we prefer to avoid, but in the end, it is that journey that brings us back. The journey is never long, though for some that journey becomes their life and in that, they lose their sense of soul and direction. It is hard—harder than I want to admit most of the time—but we can't live, looking in the rearview mirror. We need to look out at the road ahead. What is behind us is behind us. We can move forward and learn from our memories. In fact, our memories should direct us to a path of enlightenment and grace. It is sad that grace and gratitude are almost lost words today. Without grace and gratitude, the sense of humanity seems futile. Sorry. It's just a path I travel briefly. It is more of a reminder of the fragility of life than anything else. Thanks for your patience, grace, and understanding."

I feel as if the weight of my thoughts has finally lifted. I smile and reach out to take Robert's hand. He gives me a gentle kiss.

"Do you want to call Marshal Mike?" he asks, handing me the phone and the charger.

My voice lightens. "I forgot I was going to do that." I dial Mike's number. The phone rings, but there is no answer. I'm confused. Could something have happened to my Marshal Mike?

Robert says, "Maybe he had to fly back to the States early. I'm sure he'll call you when he gets a free moment."

I know he is trying to convince me not to worry. *He's probably right. Things do come up, and I certainly would not be on the top of Mike's priority list.* "I'll try later."

Robert asks what the plans are for tonight—are we going with Sonya—for some reason, I can't make a plan. I know Sonya will arrive and expect to have dinner with me. My mind now focuses on the moment. The twilight is beautiful. I will wait to make a decision on the evening. I want to take in the beauty of the hallowed land. The warm gentle breeze embraces me.

"I feel as if I'm in a Michelangelo painting. Robert says.

"Robert we are in a Michelangelo painting. I never realized that the sky was truly as he painted it until I first came to the countryside. I had imagined the images were mere fantasy, but now Ai realize this is and was reality."

"Giovanna, I want to thank you, thank you for opening my eyes to this wonderful country. You brought a new depth to my understanding of true beauty. Do you remember when I first came to visit for your birthday, and we all to a trip to Montepuciano, to the winery?"

"Robert, how could I ever forget that?"

"I remember I drove, and I think Peter and Gary were following. There were eight of us in all, if I remember correctly. We parked outside the wall in a remote parking spot. I'm not sure I really believed it was a proper parking spot. I thought you had just accidentally found a vacant piece of land that looked as if you could park a car. The walk up to the town was like mountain climbing. I thought the town was deserted. It was around lunchtime, and everyone was at home having lunch. I could smell the aromas of lunch, but had no idea where or who was doing the cooking. It was the first time I truly had walked through history. I felt embarrassed that I had never before experienced living history. The town was so remarkable. The Medici well—I was in disbelief. The Medici's had dug a well down hundreds of feet. It was an overwhelming engineering feat. We had a great lunch in the piazza. I think we scared the locals when we sat down. Eight crazy Americans, and if I remember correctly, you were the only woman. Knowing what I know now about this country and the culture that must have really stirred everyone's curiosity. The food was fantastic and so cheap. I think each of us paid five euros for a three course lunch, and that included the service charge. I remember two things: Delvin barking like a dog and you being so embarrassed you wanted to crawl under the table, and then the winery. Do you remember what happened? We had finished the self-guided tour through the old Etruscan caves and arrived at a small tasting room. I remember there was a middle-aged American couple talking with the owner and sampling some wine. We were about to leave, and the shopkeeper looked over and said, 'One moment.' He went back to the American couple, rang up their purchase and was bidding them good-bye. It was at that moment he reached over to the wife for a good-bye kiss. He moved in then stuck his tongue in her mouth. I thought her husband would have a heart attack, and she would faint. It was beyond hysterical. The look of disgust on her face, I will never forget. The smile on the Italian shopkeeper was priceless. There was a self-fulfillment about his conquest that was pure delight. If I remember correctly, you also invited that couple to your birthday party. You knew them for ten minutes and you invited them to your party. Zoe and Gabrielle are right—you are crazy.

I broke in with complete laughter. That was a perfect day and a perfect example of how Italian men will get their way. It's always best to hold the head of an Italian man when you are giving a good-bye kiss. It can save the surprise of the Italian tongue. I realize Sonya would be arriving shortly. "Should we move down to the table outside? Sonya will be here; we can all sit together."

"I'll meet you downstairs in a minute. I just want to sit here for a moment longer and embrace the twilight."

The air is full of spring; the smell of flowers and herbs fills the house. I look through our purchases from the market and put together two small platters. I set the outdoor table with glasses, plates, water, and a bottle of wine. The sun has not kissed the earth quite yet; a few tranquil moments before day will become night. Beethoven has finished playing, and I go inside to change the CD.

Robert calls from upstairs, "Giovanna, let's listen to some jazz, if you don't mind."

"*Perfecto.*"

It is time to become less pensive and more jovial. The music fills the house and the outside garden. I take a deep breath, wanting to hold on to this moment forever. Robert descends the stair. As I watch him, a revelation rises through my soul.

"Robert, this is my heaven on earth. It is as if here I live through my soul and my spirit. Things just don't matter or get in the way. The urgency of life is lost. It's about life in the moment, life as life is meant to be appreciated." We walk outside and sit watching the sun prepare to end the day. I raise my glass of wine. "A toast to Rinny, a toast to her wonderful life, *salute.*" I smile. I had the opportunity to share great joy with her and I am eternally grateful.

The phone rings. I hope Robert has the phone and that another search party is not needed.

He smiles and pulls the phone from his pocket. "Looking for this, my dear?"

It is Sonya. She says she will come tomorrow, as her plans have changed. I hang up and relay Sonya's message. That is the beauty of having a plan in Italy," I tell Robert. "There really isn't a plan, and no one will be disappointed."

We sit silently, holding hands. The amber glow of the lights of the nearby villages begins to fill the early evening darkness.

"I think I should tend to the fire," Robert says as he rises from his seat. "The night air is still a little chilly."

"You just love having a fire. That will be perfect. I'll take the food in, and we can decide what to do for dinner. If you want, we can stay here. I'll cook dinner, or we can go to town. Or if you want, we can drive over to Chiusi and have dinner at your Grill of the Forest—your restaurant."

I could see him smile at the thought of Grill of the Forest. He goes off to tend the fire. I clear the table.

I pour two glasses of water and go into the living room. The fire is ablaze.

We sit down, and doze off; the sound of jazz fills the room.

I awake to the phone ringing, half startled and lost. *Where is that phone?* The ringing leads me to the kitchen.

"*Pronto.*"

"Joann or Giovanna?" The voice is unfamiliar.

"*Si, sono Giovanna e Joann.*" I can't image who is speaking.

"It's me, Mike. How are you doing?"

"Mike! Great. What happened to you? Is everything all right? I worried when I couldn't reach you, and you didn't show up at the train station."

He laughs. "You don't have to worry. I'm a marshal, remember? I received a call from my sister. She was expecting a baby in three weeks, but as it turned out, while we were traveling across the Atlantic, she was in labor. After I called you, I received the call and headed back on a flight later that day. I didn't want to call you. I figured you'd be sleeping."

"Did she have a boy or a girl? Is everyone doing all right?"

"She had a girl, and everyone is fine. I guess someone just did the math wrong on her due date. What I wanted you to know is that my sister loves jazz, and Lena Horne is one of her favorites. She named the baby Lena, and she was born on the twenty-third. You really can't make this up. This is more than just a coincidence. When are you flying home?"

"That is not only crazy but unbelievable. I'm going home in ten days on the later flight. Are you going to be coming over anytime soon? If you are, why don't you come up to the farm? I can take you to the small villages of the Umbria countryside."

"I will be over next week and give you a call. Take care. I just had to let you know. I'll see you in a week. Ciao."

"Ciao. See you soon."

My talking has awakened Robert.

"Who's on the phone?" he asks.

"Marshal Mike." I tell him the story. We both sit silently, looking into the fire.

Robert breaks the silence. "It's as if you two were meant to be together on that flight. Something you two shared was meant to be."

I nod my head and remain silent.

Robert asks, "How long were we asleep? Do you know what time it is?"

I laugh, "There are no clocks in the house. I rely on the church bells, but I was asleep. Oh, but the phone can give us the time." After checking the time, I say with surprise, "It's eight-thirty. I guess we were tired. Are you hungry for your favorite Italian dish, or do you want to walk to the café and have a pizza? I'm thinking we should go out. I don't mind cooking tonight. I just don't want to do the clean-up, and besides, we can celebrate Rinny and the new baby Lena,"

Robert agrees.   "Grill of the Forest, and I'll do the driving so you can rest, my dear."

I glare at him in mock annoyance. "If you say 'my dear' one more time, you, my dear, will be left at the train station with a ticket to Termini. 'My dear' is for wives or ex-wives."

"Yes, dear," he spurts out.

It takes us a few minutes to gather our senses and belongings. Robert goes upstairs to change his clothes. I walk outside and look up at the night sky. The stars are brilliant, and the villages are alive. A car is driving down a distant road, and its headlight creates an eerie sense of loneliness—a lone car on a dark country road. It looks as if it is moving without specific direction. The road twists back on itself, making the image seem surreal. The evening breeze is strong, and the rustle of the olive branches fills the air. The birds are quiet. The smell of smoke from the fireplace fills the outside air. The music has stopped, and now playing are the sounds of nature. I walk back inside. The house is warm and the fire embers cast an okra glow across the room. Robert returns from upstairs, and we are off. As we drive down the driveway, I notice he has left the light on in the sitting room upstairs.

"Robert, Rose will be calling you on the light you left on. Do you want to go back and turn it off?"

"Maybe she will think we are upstairs resting."

"That's your cross to bear with Rose. I'm staying clear. You have been warned and advised."

We drive through Chiusi and on to the small restaurant just outside of town. It is a small bed-and-breakfast with a dining room. As we walk in, we see an open fireplace for grilling. The aromas of the cooking meats fill the air, and the darkly lit dining room seems more like a private space, as if we've been invited to a friend's house for dinner. The room is full with six tables, each having a variety of chairs and flatware. The owner, Anthony, greets us. He and his wife run the entire operation, and their three-year-old son entertains the guests with his laughter. Sophia, Anthony's wife, comes over and greets us. We hug and kiss. She asks how long we will stay in Italy and why we have been gone for so long. I usually try to visit more often, but things just got in the way. When I'm here, time seems to stand still. I never want to leave. I can't ever imagine going back. *Someday, I promise myself, I will stay here, and I will visit the other side of the pond for short stays.*

I've told my children and Robert that when I'm old, they should put me in the olive grove, and when the owl lands on my head, my time will have ended. My children have taunted me, saying they will put me in an old folks' home and never come to visit. I've assured them if that is the case, I will haunt them forever. So it will be the olive grove for me. I realize that Sophia is directing us to sit down. I apologize for not paying attention. Robert shakes his finger at me.

"Pinch me," I say to him. "It's like traveling to another dimension. It's like a parallel life. Knowing this exists at the same time my parallel crazy life exists defies reason. There are parallel lives, but few people are lucky enough to experience them—some by choice and some out of ignorance. Here, my body is part of the earth and nature. I remember when I was little, and we would be with my father's family. I'm not sure how to explain this, but it is as if the time we were apart disappears, and only the time we are together is real. I guess it's like a dream—when you are in a dream, nothing else matters but your dream, and reality vanishes the moment you awake. When I leave Italy, I bring her with me. When I leave the States, I leave it all behind. It's like a dream that vanishes, and I don't miss it."

"You don't leave it all behind," Robert says, "because I know how much you love your children, and you don't leave them behind."

I think for a moment and respond, "I don't leave my children behind. They come with me when I am here. I feel them more here than when I am back in the States. There is too much clutter in everyday life. We forget; we have a list of to-dos a mile long, and we forget. Here, they are with me, and when they come and are physically here with me, that is a gift from God. I cherish those moments more than anything else. The fact that I have been able to allow them to see part of what my childhood was is the greatest gift I can give them. That's what is painful—not having Rinny here. I can't give her that gift, and that truly breaks my heart." Tears fill my eyes, and we are silent. The sounds of the restaurant fill my pounding, sorrowful heart.

Sophia and her son come over to the table. He climbs up on my lap, and I give him a kiss, telling him I have missed him. He smiles and jumps off my lap and onto Robert. He repeats the kiss and hug, and then he's off to entertain another guest. Robert's dream meal will be wild boar, deer, and rabbit—tonight's grill of the forest. As he orders, a smile comes over his face. I will have the ravioli. We order water and a glass of house wine to finish the meal.

Robert says, "Can I tell you a story?"

"Only if it's a happy one."

"Okay, here is a happy story for you. When I was a little boy, in the summer, we lived on the island and went to church every Sunday morning. I remember your dad in his blue suit, but my most vivid memory was after church, when your mother and my mother would talk for what appeared to be an eternity. I wanted to get home and take my suit off. Remember those days, when every male wore a suit to church?"

I nodded.

"Well, our mothers would just keep talking, and I wanted to run home and get out of that suit so bad. I had to wear a suit every day in Catholic school. Saturday and part of Sunday were my only suit-free days. I wanted to play with my friends. But my mom wouldn't let me cross the parking lot to go home. We lived a hundred yards away, but I had to stand there and listen to these two women talk. I'd beg my mother to let me go. The more I begged, the tighter she held my hand. Then your mother would look at me and say, 'Don't act like a brat.' I couldn't believe she said that to me. My mother looked at me and said, 'You don't want people to think you are a brat.' I really didn't care if anyone thought I was a brat. I just wanted to get out of my suit. What I wanted to do was just stick my tongue out at your mother."

I begin to laugh hysterically and said, "While you were trying to get out of your suit and play, we were all waiting in the car to do the same thing. Only we wanted to go to Aunt Lena and Uncle Nick's. We should have had an Italian plan." I continue to laugh.

Robert picks up where he left off. "Well, the worst of the story was that when they finally parted, my mother looked at me with those eyes that say only one thing: *Wait until your father gets home.* That made me want to stick my tongue out at my mother. I was so mad. When we reached our lawn at the end of the church parking lot, I pulled away from her and ran as fast as I could into the house. I thought if I was fast, I could get out the door before she made it to the porch. I wasn't fast enough."

I interrupt, "Did you get a spanking?"

"No. I was coming downstairs when she came in the house. I could hear the door slam. It always slammed and still does to this day. She told me to never be rude again. The only thing I could do was promise I wouldn't be rude. From that point on, anytime I saw your mother coming to talk to my mother, I would always tell my mom I had to go the bathroom. It worked like a charm. I never had to stand there listening to the two of them chatter. That's my story, and I'm sticking to it."

I clap my hands and say, "Bravo. Did your mom tell your dad?"

"No. Irish guilt took over. I apologized and said I would never do it again. That worked."

"That's why I wouldn't hang out with you, because I knew you were a brat. My mother must have told me that." I can't stop laughing.

"Giovanna, you are so funny. The reason you wouldn't talk or hang out with me when we were young was because you are so much older than I am." He puts his hands over his mouth, trying to hold back the laughter.

"Shut up. I'm not that much older than you. You make me crazy when you say that. We are only eighteen months apart, not eighteen years, or better yet, not the fifteen years difference between my mom and dad. Remember when I was a photographer for the high school newspaper and yearbook? I actually let you have my sacred Nikon to photograph the school's basketball team. When I developed the film, I realized not one image was in focus."

Robert breaks in. "I didn't have my glasses with me. I did the best I could. That was over thirty-five years ago. Are you still going to hold that grudge?" he asks and then ends with, "My dear."

I can't take it anymore. I break into laughter. "You are making my stomach hurt from laughing. I think we need to cut your storytelling days short, my dear."

Sophia returns to the table with our dinner. She hands Robert the large sword, which doubles as a knife, to cut through the "Grill of the Forest." The dinner plate is a bounty of carnivore delight. I look at Robert and say, "It's a manly meal. *Buon appetito.*"

"Do you want to try some manly men's meat?"

I almost spit out the water in my mouth. Robert begins to laugh. I look around the dining room, thankful most of the dinner guests have left. Looking him in the eye, I say, "It's a wonderful thing that the owners are my friends. Otherwise, we would most likely be out the door by now."

"Can I please tell you another story?" Robert pleads.

"I'm not sure right now. Can I get back to you with an answer?"

He begs, "Just one more story. I promise."

"Don't quit your day job. Oh, we are waiting to see if you have a day job." He glances at me slightly hurt. I shake my head and say, "Listen. We might be in Dublin eating boiled meat and potatoes six ways. So enjoy the moment, and don't look so insulted. No one has ever tried harder to find a job. When the right one comes along, then it's 'Grill of the Forest' all around. Start your story."

"Before I start my story, can I ask one question?"

"So is that your question?" I tease.

"No, here is my question. Is tomorrow Sunday? If tomorrow is Sunday, we don't have to work in the grove. We can go to Arezzo and see Sarah and Pietro. Right?"

I think for a moment. "Tomorrow is definitely Sunday. You're right about not working on Sunday. There is at least one exception to that rule that I am aware of. During the olive harvest, everyone works every day. God gives us a forgiveness pass. I don't know if that means pruning allows you the God-forgiveness pass. I think it's Sunday, and so it's to Arezzo we will go. I know what you are thinking. You're thinking Pietro will make lunch, but it's much too late to call Sarah and Pietro. We can call in the morning. I know your love for driving in Italy. You can drive. We can bring Sarah and Zara back with us from Arezzo. She can take the train back to Arezzo the next day. *Bravo*. We now have another Italian plan in place. Okay, and now for your story."

Robert holds up his hand. "Excuse me. Can we take the Autostrada up? We can take 71 back. Please." He was truly begging. For Robert, driving on the Autostrada is his dream come true. It is the ultimate macho driving experience.

I smile and chuckle. "The Autostrada up and SS71 down sounds perfect, now, will you tell me your story?"

"The story?"

"Yes, the story you were about to tell."

Sophia and Anthony's son runs to our table and jumps in my lap. We laugh. He jumps down and runs into Robert's lap. The dining room is now empty with the exception of Robert and me. I pour the last of the water into our glasses.

Robert starts to talk. "This isn't the story, but it is something I was thinking about on the plane. You know how you always say be Zen and that the universe can better handle the hurdles in life. Well, being an Irish Catholic, I must confess I thought you were crazy. I don't want to downplay your insanity, but there is more to what you say than I had ever thought before. Now, I will tell you my story. Remember when you first invited me to your birthday party?" He touches my hand, and I nod. "Well, a lot had happened in my life from the initial invitation to my actual acceptance. The specifics are not important. What is important is that for some reason, and I'm sure God knows, I accepted at the last minute. After booking my flight, I realized I was traveling internationally, for the first time on my own, to a country whose language I didn't speak, and I had no idea where I was going. When I arrived in Roma, I realized that language no longer mattered, because I couldn't understand it. My hearing lessened, and my vision became heightened. The analogy I can give you is someone dropping you off at the Island ferry and saying, 'Here you are.' Here is where? I don't have an address; I don't have anything. Here is here. But where is here? You know the story of the *Carabinieri* and my frantic calls to tell you where I was and my hopes of knowing where I was going. It was surreal for me. I had decided in less than twelve hours to take this journey. I booked my ticket and had a map with me that you had drawn on a napkin. After Termini, I thought it could only get better. I called you with my location and arrival time. I sat on the train and looked out at the landscape and in that vista; there was a sense of awe. Then I arrived at the Chiusi train station. For the first ten minutes, time slowed down; my eyes and brain were racing. I couldn't speak because I didn't know what to say. If I did know what to say, I couldn't say it. My brain brought me back to a safe haven, the Summit train station in New Jersey. I looked around the station. It was full of teenage children. There was a sense of confusion, but it was the sense of standing among this group of youth that becalmed me. The train station in Chiusi was different than it is today—it was less congested. I scanned the street, hoping to see you. Then finally, I looked up, and you were running across the street in front of the taxi stand. At that moment when I heard you call my name, everything made sense. You ran over and hugged me. It closed a loop for me and created an instant connection. Do you remember that you apologized so much for being late as we walked over to the car? When we arrived, Pietro emerged. He greeted me with kindness, and the first words out of his mouth were 'Sit in the front.' I was humbled by his kindness. As we were driving, you asked how things had been going. I had to let everything out; no one had asked in so long, it was time to let go. What was strange was that Pietro was in the backseat.

I had only met him for two minutes, and yet I felt completely comfortable pouring my heart and woes out. When I finished, I remember Pietro suggested we stop in Cetona at the local workers' bar. It was at that point I realized he understood my pain and the need to stop for a moment to afford me the liberty to gather my thoughts.

"When we arrived at the bar, I was taken aback by how austere the bar was with the large wooden tables. It was Italian home-grown, but it seemed to lack any sense of hospitality. I truly was bringing my Americanism with me. Pietro ordered wine for us, and we sat outside. I began to see the hospitality of Italy. It is so subtle that one has to be open to see it. Pietro was so kind, and speaking with the two of you gave me a haven, a place within myself where I could be comfortable. You know me, and you know I have dealt with many situations in the corporate world. I'm not inexperienced or unable to cope, but the two of you gave me a foundation to stand on. To be perfectly honest, it took a few moments to actually absorb the new surroundings. Do you understand what I'm trying to say?"

I squeezed his hand. "I understand. The mental and emotional torture people put each other through is not comprehensible to Pietro or me. That is why it was easy to be together and to create a haven for you to spill out your soul. You were just learning."

Robert resumed. "I remember the drive to the house. There was laughter in the car. It was the first time I had heard laughter in such a long time. I wanted to cry. I realized what had been missing for so long in my life—kindness, love, and laughter. After my confession, neither of you judged me. You merely wanted to make a sanctuary for me. I thank both of you for that. When we arrived at the house, I remember walking in and thinking, *Who are all these people? Where do they live?* You introduced everyone to me and then added, they all have homes on the Island. I thought to myself, *I have never rubbed elbows with any of these people. I have lived on Shelter Island all my life, at least in the summers. Who are these people and how could I have been so disconnected from them?* When you introduced me to Kelly, and she looked at me and said, 'I know you,' I literally froze in my steps. I had seen her before, but I just couldn't place it. You know the feeling you get when you meet someone that you previously met, and you are not sure if the previous meeting was amicable? She was a real estate agent who might have had a buyer for my house. I wasn't uncomfortable. We talked about the meeting—we shared my angst. At the time, I had not an inclination of where this would all lead. However, it would be a lie if I didn't tell you my world was changing.

"The next moment of complete enchantment was Pietro's lunch, which was truly an epicurean delight. I, having thought I was knowledgeable of the world, became lost in what was pure nirvana. The table was as long as a football field. People were bustling, and Pietro was completely in charge. It was Pietro's offering. I swear I will never forget that moment. There must have been at least twelve or fifteen of us, and there was not a moment of chaos. I felt as if I had walked into a movie set with a demographic of people I had overlooked for over twenty years. I will openly admit that I was never afforded the opportunity to be in a home in a foreign country. For the first time, my reserve was completely lost. When I looked around the table, everyone was there for one reason, and that reason truly was to celebrate Giovanna. I think we ate so much, no one could move.

"But now, I look back at going to sleep that night. You provided me with a beautiful haven. I was slightly overwhelmed at the entire day's events and took your first offering. I was uncertain. Sleeping in the Italian countryside, miles from any town, was remarkable. The whole day was remarkable. I remember hearing sounds outside, not realizing at the time what significance they had. I awoke, only to find out the next morning it was the call of the wild boar. The entire journey for me was life-altering. I knew I had just developed a lasting relationship. Yet at the time, I hadn't really understood its true depth. I realize now, not only did I fall in love with Italy, but I fell in love with you. The only thing I knew at the time was that it all felt good. When we were all dancing at the party the next night, it was as if everyone in that room had a connection. Gary said it best when he made a toast to you for your birthday. His toast was about the relevancy of sharing the moment, reflecting how you had brought everyone together. What he said that night resonates in my head when I think of you. You have an innate ability to bring people together and to show them what is important in life. Watching you is amazing; you don't even realize you are doing it. It's been a while since that night, and everyone at that party has become even closer to you and to me. It is similar to what you were saying before. When you leave Italy, you bring it with you, and when you return, it is as if you never left. That is the way I feel about everyone I met at that moment. We all brought baggage. We all left cleansed. What really makes me crazy is you don't see it. For you, it's your life. I remember the first time I walked into your house on the island. I thought, *This woman has no furniture or stuff.* I asked you about it, and the word was, 'We have what we need; it's all about Zen. Stuff is stuff; don't get lost in it. I have the silver and the plates but unlike most, we use them every day. Why have special accruements. Every moment is special.' It's ironic that it was your birthday, and it is ironic that we are here together to remember Rinny's birthday. Your children have the same kind of humanity you have, which is why I am here two days early. When the festivities of your birthday were over, I felt a sense of loss. I was lost for one reason—I didn't understand the bond you share with your friends. As I see it, everyone is together, and no man or woman is left behind. Do you understand? It's today, celebrating Rinny, and knowing she will always be gone. Now everything makes sense. You woke a genie in me that had long lain dormant. Life then was more like a treadmill. I worked, waiting to achieve retirement age and a home in Florida. Where would that lead? How could I survive? I remember my flight back to America after the celebration was over. My flight was later than yours.

You dropped us off at the terminal and returned the rental car. I kissed you good-bye and headed to my gate. It seemed that everyone kissed and hugged. When I arrived, that was foreign, but when I left, it was pedestrian. I still was not aware of how life-changing this event was. I remember sitting at the airport gate, and I felt a hand over my eyes. It was you. I was so touched that you just wanted to check and make sure everything was all right. What it all comes down to is that the small moments, the moments that are not planned, end up being the ones that cause major change in our lives. There is nothing more truthful than the statements, 'A moment changes everything' and 'Life turns on a dime.' Somehow or other, you obtained that understanding a long time ago. I see your mission here as more of a teacher than a student on a path. You teach everyone around you to value the goodness of life and the moment. As you often say, there is no guarantee that you will have another moment to live. You also taught me never to be afraid—the universe and God by any name will take care of you, and you are right. Thank you."

I sat for a moment, completely lost for words. "You give me much more credit than I ever deserve. Tragedy makes one really look deep into the meaning of everything—not just the moment but all moments. When we lost Rinny, it seemed as if life stopped, and the world stood still. I knew from that moment on that life would never be the same. Death causes life to never be the same. I had to find strength, not for me but for my children. The person I looked to for that was Rinny and my faith. I knew more than anything that my children needed me, and in that, I found strength. We all pulled together and the canyon of pain gradually filled. We are taught that death is the end, and life the beginning In fact, neither is either. Once you can grasp that thought and hold it, you will understand it is the moments that are the beginning and the end."

I am rambling. I am slightly overwhelmed. We realize, at that moment, Sophia is coming to our table. *Il conto*. We bid good night and kiss. Walking to the car, holding hands and looking through the dark night, we find a silent comfort. Inside the car, Robert leans over and kisses me.

On the drive home, I fall into sleep.

Chapter 12
Haven

The sound of the earth rubbing against the car frame wakes me.

"Sorry—I fell asleep on the drive home."

"As long as one of us is awake, we're safe." Robert parks the car in the designated Rose parking spot. "I didn't forget Rose's words of advice regarding the proper parking area. Since tomorrow is Sunday, can we go to mass at Santa Maria del Grazie? I love listening to Don Enrico's mass. He seems to put so much life and vitality into every word he says. I think I could use a spiritual experience."

I look over at him. "I'm up for mass here anytime. I love the voices as they resonate through the church. The light cascading through the windows illuminates the dark corners. The church just comes to life. The pews are so tiny; I don't know how you sit on them. I'd love to go to mass with you tomorrow."

We sit silently for a few moments in the little Fiat, overlooking the dark fields. Off in the distance, we can see the late train to Roma, a stream of light breaking the darkness.

"Giovanna, what time is mass tomorrow?"

I think for a moment. "It starts at 10 a.m., I think. Don't worry. The church bells will toll when it's time to arrive."

Robert opens the car door and says, "It's time to head inside.

197

Remember, I told you the girls gave me something for you. I'll start the upstairs fire, and we can relax for a few minutes. Does that work for you?"

I wait to see if he will open my door. It is more a test of his chivalry than anything else. Earlier in town, he opened the car door; I was suspicious that it was a male display for the local men. Now, Robert closes his car door and heads to the house.

"Hey, baby, are you leaving me in the car tonight?" I call after him. "I was skeptical in town when you opened the car door for me, and now my suspicions are confirmed."

"I thought you were a self-made woman with liberal feminist leanings. Not to mention your spiritual beliefs," he calls back and continues to walk to the house.

"That doesn't mean you can't be polite."

He stops walking for a second, turns around, and looks right at me. "I'm waiting to open the door to the house. I thought you could handle the door to the car." Then he walks to the door of the house and holds it open.

I open the car door and say, "Good save. Good save, my dear."

We both break into laughter and enter the house. Robert retreats upstairs to light the fire. I wander into the kitchen to get a bottle of water and two glasses. I can see that the earlier fire in the living room is just now beginning to fade. I call up to Robert, "Do you want anything from the kitchen?"

I realize he can't hear me. I shut off the kitchen light and ascend the stairway to join him. Upstairs, the fire is beginning to ignite. Robert is crouching over the hearth with his fire poker, pushing the logs this way and that. It seems men always have to poke a fire. They can never just light the fire and let it burn. I attribute it to some primordial throwback of the earlier hunting and gathering days of homo sapiens. I sit down on the couch and pour us each a glass of water. Watching the fire, I realize how amazing it is. The fireplace is merely the two walls of the house. The thick stone walls are the firebox, and its white walls show only slight traces of smoke. The fireplace was so efficiently designed—a marriage of form and function. Robert pokes at the fire a few more times and then sits down next to me. I hand him his water and kiss him on the cheek.

"Can you read to me from the *History of Italy* book?" I ask.

"Of course I can. Where can I find it?"

"It's on the desk behind us. I'll get it." I shake my head, remembering he used up all of his chivalry for the day. I walk over to the desk and pick up the antique tome and think to myself, *How many have held this in their hands and read through these pages?* I walk back over and hand the tome to Robert.

"Where would you like to start? Dark Ages, Burning of Roma, Medici murder?"

"You're reading; you pick."

He leafs through the pages and stops, "The Etruscans."

I curl up, and he begins to read as I watch the flames building. He read for half an hour and then stops and looks over at me. "Remember when you took me to Volterra."

I smile. "One of my favorite places. The town is so beautiful. Remember the museum with the funerary urns? The expressions on each of the sculptured faces are more than their expression; each was actually a portrait, and the small carvings around the bases. I can't imagine how anyone could sculpt so delicately. Remember the depictions of the battles, the heroic events in an individual's life? The best is having the works displayed so you truly can see and experience them. I had to hold back from wanting to touch them. When we went outside to the small garden area, there were fragments of art lying on the ground. It was as if we were walking through an antique disposal site for unwanted pieces or quality unacceptable. It reminded me of an ancient artist studio graveyard. I can still see those images in my mind."

Robert breaks in. "I can remember the light in the room and the slightest scent of dampness. I imagine that the scent was the same then as it is today. No heat. The stone must have been frigid. Yet the artist carved life and warmth into them. Volterra, to me, is a city that was of profound political and social importance. It was one of the twelve leading Etruscan centers in Italy. When we walked through the town, it held that same magical quality—the churches, museums, and the streets. One day I would love to go and spend the night, to walk the streets at twilight and watch the town burst into animation. However, that being said, the craziest and most unexpected exhibit was the traveling exhibit of torture devices.'

I break in, "I wouldn't even go up to the entrance. I remember it well,"

Robert continues. "Once I walked to the entrance and saw the horrific machinery designed specifically to torture—humans against humans—I was repelled by some force. That is when I turned around and walked away."

"What type of mind can intentionally and willfully inflict so much physical pain on another human?" My voice sounds so confused.

Robert puts the book down and looks at me. "Giovanna, the depth of torture is not only physical, as you well know. Torture comes mentally as well. It is still used today by what we endearingly call civilized societies. Only our governments are much better at hiding it. We only learn of it when some cocky individual who was part of the horror starts to brag. What's even worse is that some even photograph the torture. I best stop here for now." Robert gets up and pokes at the fire. He turns and says, "Do you have an electrical converter upstairs?"

I think a moment. This might be a trick question to see if I have things in order. I answer, "There should be one in the desk drawer. If it's not—"

"Then you mean it could be anywhere. Oh, Giovanna."

He walks over to the desk and right where it should be, it is. One lucky break for me. He heads toward the bedroom and closes the door.

I call out to him, "What are you doing in there? Is it time for bed?" I hear rattling and turn back to look at the fire. The house is still, the crackling of the fire the only sound present. I know it must be late, and we probably should head off to bed. I place the tome back on the desk and turn the lights off. As I open the door to the bedroom, I see Robert bent over on the floor.

"What are you doing? Are you all right?" I ask anxiously.

"I'm fine. I'm just putting something together. Is it bedtime? I'll be done in a minute."

I head for the bathroom to clean up. When I finish, I open the bathroom door and jump into bed. Robert is just finishing unpacking some clothes and heads off to the bathroom. From the bed, I can see the fire burning. I am living my dream, and I am grateful. I always promise in the morning and at night that I will always say thank-you to the universe.

Robert comes into the bedroom and says, "I have something for you from your girls. Are you ready? They say this is a tradition." He climbs into bed and reaches over onto the floor. He pulls up an old-fashioned video camera. "Zoe and Gabrielle told me you would watch this on Rinny's birthday every year, and they wanted to keep the tradition alive."

I freeze.

"Hey, are you going to be okay?" he asks. He pushes the play button. On the tiny little screen I see Rinny and then her voice. A smile comes over my face. I look over at Robert and say, "I'm better than okay. That's my Rinny."

We watch the video and at one point during the Jerry Springer spoof, Robert looks over, laughing as hard as he can, and says, "This is so funny. Rinny was a riot. Did she and her friend just do this on the fly, or was there a plan?" He can barely speak.

"The plan, as always in Rinny's life, was do it on the fly." At the end of the video was a segment of Rinny riding the horse she had always wanted to purchase. Yes, I did buy her that horse.

Robert asks, "Is that Bingo?"

"Absolutely, none other."

"He must be a hundred by now. Zoe still is taking care of him." There is disbelief in his voice.

"That's our Bingo—Rinny's dream and Zoe's reality."

The video ends, and Robert gets out of bed to place the camera on the dresser. "She was pretty amazing, that Rinny." When he climbs back in bed, we hold each other in silence.

"Robert, you know what I was just thinking about? The only event in life that puts a stop to everything is death. Think about it. Say you want some friends or family to visit. Usually there are ten reasons that they can't make the journey, and the visit is postponed. The only event that stops time is death. The minute we hear of the death of someone we love, we stop everything and make every attempt to go to help. Whatever plans are made seem trite. Our entire focus is on the individual who just passed and those closest to the person who is still standing. Nothing has such an impact as death. Birth—we have months to plan for a birth, and our schedules are worked around that. Death gives no indicators, even for those terminally ill. If a doctor tells you that you have three month to live, what do you do? You probably change your life around, making the most out of the last three months, but the doctor can't guarantee you those three months. The only guarantee from death is death itself. I feel sad that so many people put off what's important. I don't mean to live a wild and freewheeling lifestyle. There is a balance. It is simple as always saying 'I love you' when you see someone or at the end of a phone conversation. Words might be the last words you speak, or the last words they speak."

Robert hugs me. "*Sogni d'oro, amore.* Golden dreams, my love."

"*Sogni d'oro, amori.*"

We kiss each other good night.

"Robert, you know what gives me the most comfort? It's that the last words Rinny ever said to me as she kissed me goodnight were 'I love you.'"

* * *

After…. I thank all of you with grace and gratitude. You have given me light.

Eyes and heart
Flooded with
Tears of
Sorrow
And
Joy.

Brazen sits on a lost soul
Imagined a voice or image
Brazen sits on a lost soul
lost

Italy called me, and I listened and returned to find safety. Now, Italy is home. Lena, Nick, and Rinny share this life with me. Happy birthday, Rinny! This statement deafens my ears and blinds me to my loss. I now look around this plane, again remembering what I try to forget each day. Rinny, I never will let you leave my heart, but I want to forget the day you left. Your life rings through the trees, the fields, and your siblings. Your last breath is truly my first, for my new world is now dark and silent without you.

CPSIA information can be obtained at www.ICGtesting.com
Printed in the USA
BVOW02*1922100715

408022BV00003B/66/P